D1244731

UNTOUCHABLE

Untouchable

Reflections on Twenty-Seven Unforgettable Years with Clint

· · · ⬠ · · ·

DON SEYMOUR

[signature]

FOREWORD BY

Roberto Clemente Jr.

SMALL BATCH BOOKS
Amherst, Massachusetts

ISBN 978-1-937650-50-6

Library of Congress Control Number: 2014960143

Book design by Simon M. Sullivan

SMALL
BATCH
BOOKS

493 SOUTH PLEASANT STREET
AMHERST, MASSACHUSETTS 01002
413.230.3943
SMALLBATCHBOOKS.COM

Dedicated to my daughter and my other hero,
Carly Seymour,
in memory of her unforgettable brother, Clint

The net proceeds from the sale of this book will be donated to
the Clint Seymour "Play Ball" Fund (clintplayball.com).

"The heroes of the past are untouchable, protected forever by the fortress door of time."

ACKNOWLEDGMENTS

To Clint's aunts, uncles, cousins, coaches, teammates, co-workers, and friends, who remain steadfastly loyal to him.

To my lifelong friend Dr. Bill McMillan, who suggested that I attempt to write this book and then flattered me into believing that I could actually accomplish it.

To my friends, too numerous to count, at the K&L Gates Pittsburgh and Charleston offices, my only home away from home since 1970, whose stars have never shone brighter.

To all the folks at Merrill Lynch (Charleston), Clint's employer for the last month of his life, led by Frank Frazier and Randy Domikis, who entered our lives in a hospital room and who have not left our hearts since.

To my friend Tom Reiter, who inspired me with his gift of prose, who has been gracious enough to laugh at my jokes over the years, and who will be compassionate enough to understand if they may not flow as easily in the future.

To my friend Melissa Tea, for editorial support.

To Niki and Neil Walker, who continue to make Clint, Carly, Mary, and me so proud of their friendship.

To the real author of this book, who directed every word from the start, My Guy.

Clint and his mother, Mary

CONTENTS

FOREWORD

---

by Roberto Clemente Jr.

I knew Clint Seymour his entire life. I have known his father, Don, most of my life. I enjoyed watching Clint grow up to eventually become the vibrant, exuberant young man that he was at the age of twenty-seven. And I also enjoyed tracking his development as a baseball player from his youth through college. You couldn't know Clint or Don without knowing the other and admiring their relationship. In one of my last conversations with Clint, he was telling me how much he valued his relationship with his parents. I told him that I understood that value more than most, reminding him that I was only seven years old when I lost my father.

I have been immersed in the game of baseball most of my life, and I have felt the impact of personal family tragedy. So when I learned that Don had written a book reflecting on Clint's life and maturity through a baseball lens, I expected it would include messages that would touch me. I was not disappointed. If you have had the good fortune of knowing Clint, Carly, Don, or Mary, each chapter will bring a smile or a tear. If you love baseball, you will be reminded of the enduring values and impact of the game. If you are a parent, some life lessons will be reinforced by a father who got it right. In any event, as Don suggests, you are certain to give those you love an extra hug.

ROBERTO CLEMENTE JR.
Houston, Texas
August 2014

ROBERTO CLEMENTE, father of Roberto Jr., was an iconic baseball player for the Pittsburgh Pirates from 1955 to 1972. He led the Pirates to two World Series championships, was the National League MVP in 1966, led the league in hitting four times, was awarded twelve gold gloves, and played in fifteen all-star games. He lost his life on New Year's Eve 1972, when a DC-7 airplane he had chartered to personally deliver earthquake relief to Nicaragua crashed into the ocean off the Puerto Rican coast. Tom Walker, a major league pitcher playing that winter for a team managed by Roberto, helped load the plane, but because Roberto wanted Tom to go celebrate New Year's Eve, he told him not to join him on the flight. Tom Walker's son Neil would become a teammate and close friend of Clint's and the Pirates second baseman and was at Clint's bedside when his life ended. Roberto became the first Latin American player to be enshrined in the Baseball Hall of Fame in 1973. The Roberto Clemente Award is presented annually by Major League Baseball to the player best combining playing skills and community service.

Roberto Jr. with Clint

PROLOGUE

On April 26, 2014, our twenty-seven-year-old son, Clint Seymour, was peacefully walking the streets of his adopted home of Charleston, South Carolina, on a lovely spring night, perfectly sober (having agreed to serve as the designated driver for his group of three that evening). It was just hours after the twenty-fifth birthday of his sister, Carly, in San Antonio, Texas, and Clint had spent much of that evening bragging to his two new acquaintances about his strong relationship with his family and his pleasure with his relocation to Charleston.

With each step he took, Clint carried a life brimming with enthusiasm and joy. Each step had been forged by loving parents, an amazing sister, devoted coaches, and a national network of teammates and friends who relied upon him for regular infusions of pure, unadulterated joy. Each step brought him inches closer to a future that was tantalizing with opportunity. But suddenly, abruptly, senselessly, there would be no more steps. Two blocks away from his car, he was the victim of an unprovoked homicide. He was ambushed by what the police have termed a "running punch," a "sucker punch" to his head from behind, a punch he never saw coming from an assailant he did not know and who probably never saw Clint's face. And as quickly as the ambush erupted, so it ceased with his assailant disappearing into the night, leaving Clint lifeless on the sidewalk. As the police later reported to us, he was, tragically, the wrong person in the wrong place at the wrong time. He had inexplicably become the latest victim of the random "one-punch homicide" that has increased at an alarming rate and has been the subject of legislative initiatives in some states, as well as in Australia ("king punch") and the United Kingdom. While dubbed "sucker punches" or "knockout punches," they also have been described accurately as "coward's punches."

The tragically short, twenty-seven-year life of my son and my hero was intertwined with baseball—directly for sixteen years and indirectly for many more. He found enjoyment and exuded enthusiasm every time he ran onto a baseball diamond. He honored the game and respected his teammates. The game rewarded him. His friends elevated him. Now I honor him.

Neil Walker, Don, Carly, Mary at PNC Park, May 10, 2014

For centuries, the world's youth have developed positive character traits and enduring friendships through countless types of structured group activities. Clint's primary outlet

"First Pitches" by Don and Carly, May 10, 2014 (Pirates vs. Cardinals)

was baseball, and so that is the vehicle through which his story is reflected.

Clint's baseball life began at a very young age, through programs in Mt. Lebanon, Pennsylvania, and the St. Louise de Marillac Catholic Church in neighboring Upper St. Clair. Those early years eventually led to a magical AAU (Amateur Athletic Union) baseball experience with the Steel City Wildcats. Clint enjoyed a highly successful high school career, playing four years with a champion Mt. Lebanon High School team and earning first-team all-state honors as an outfielder in 2004. Then came the BP/Bulldogs, who won national amateur baseball championships in two consecutive years. Clint also played fall baseball with the Mid-Atlantic Rookies during his high school years. His baseball experience culminated with four years as a Division I scholarship player at Eastern Kentucky University.

The remaining six years of Clint's short life would be a testament to the impact that baseball had upon his character. He continued to mature. He found other outlets for his athletic talents, including running and golf. His positive qualities blossomed. The self-discipline and the respect and the determination shaped on the baseball diamond served him very well. Even more lasting, however, was the inner joy baseball had ingrained in him over many years. Clint freely shared this with all whose lives he touched.

Jumbotron tribute to Clint at PNC Park, May 10, 2014 (Pirates vs. Cardinals)

Indeed, Clint provided the Clint Seymour "Play Ball" Fund (clintplayball.com), which was established in his honor, with the template for its mission:

> *"No one plays baseball forever. Yet, the lessons learned last an eternity. Among those lessons, none is more valuable than the capacity to bring joy to others, the most precious gift bestowed by baseball."*

We created the fund to continue Clint's legacy, and to enable other children to experience the same positive impact the game of baseball had on the development of Clint's character and personality, by providing young baseball players with opportunities to nurture enduring character traits such as self-discipline, respect, determination, and self-esteem. The fund will fulfill its mission—initially in Pennsylvania and South Carolina—through funding for facilities for safe and enjoyable youth baseball experiences and through programs and publications intended to perpetuate the joy of baseball and its opportunities for positive character development.

Brian Seymour's Pittsburgh eulogy captured a perceptive thought that motivates Clint's "Play Ball" Fund:

"We rejoice in the knowledge that, freed from his restrictive, material body, he now has the ability to impact the world and those he loved in ways far more powerful and more meaningful than would have otherwise been possible."

The fund's original board of directors includes Thomas Birsic, Walker Coleman, Andrew Goff, Alex Grover, Tyler Haak, Thomas Reiter, Charles Rudek, Mark Saghy, Brian Seymour, Carly Seymour, Dixon Seymour, Donald Seymour, James Seymour, Richard Seymour, and Neil Walker.

Clint's legacy also includes the impact of his decision to be an organ donor. Four lives were saved. His heart never stopped beating and now lives in North Carolina; his liver is in Kentucky; and his kidneys went to two recipients in South Carolina. Anyone with an adult child or spouse should encourage him or her to make a decision—whatever it may be—on the subject, so as not to burden the next of kin with that decision in an imperfect setting. Those four lives might not have been saved had it not been for the fact that we knew Clint was registered as an organ donor, a decision that Mary and I immediately respected.

Visit organdonor.gov to find out more about becoming an organ donor.

Untouchable is published for Clint's many friends and the descendants of Clint's family (since tragically he now will have none of his own)—descendants who may never have had a chance to meet him, but who can still be touched by his life. It is written primarily in the first-person singular. It is also written, however, on behalf of Mary, my wife of twenty-nine years and Clint's mother. Clint was born six days before our first anniversary, so he has been a part of virtually all of our married life. As you may infer from these pages, Mary has been—and remains—a devoted, loving parent of Clint every day of his life on Earth and thereafter. We all grieve differently. My mechanisms are more external, whereas hers are more private. The process of creating this book would have been agonizing for Mary. I chose to spare her that pain. But the reader may be assured that many of the sentiments expressed herein are Mary's, shared more privately, and that no one could possibly love our son more. And no sibling could love a brother more than his sister and our daughter, Carly—my other hero—to whom I dedicate this book and the rest of my life.

DON SEYMOUR
August, 2014

Our family at the wedding of Charlie and Kate Seymour

ONE

The Luckiest Man on the Face of the Earth

"So, Clint," she said, "when am I going to see that house of yours, the one with the marsh views over to Bohicket Creek?"

"Oh, you won't believe it. On a clear day, you can see all the way to the Edisto Bridge."

"Well, let's go, babe, it's a clear, sunny day. I'm tired of hearing about it."

As Clint pulled into the driveway, she noticed two cars in the garage.

"I thought you said you lived here by yourself."

Without missing a beat, Clint deadpanned, "Well, I let my parents stay here occasionally."

"I consider myself the luckiest man on the face of the Earth." Aware that he was suffering from an incurable disease, Lou Gehrig provided the Yankee Stadium crowd on July 4, 1939, the paradoxical quote that became one of the most recognized of the twentieth century. He conveyed to his fans that, while he recognized his time on this Earth would be shorter than most, he could nonetheless assure them that—as a result of the fulfillment of his baseball dreams and the adoration of his fans—he considered himself "the luckiest man on the face of the Earth."

Having lost his life at age twenty-seven to a senseless, un-

1

provoked, and inexplicable homicide, Clint can hardly be regarded as the luckiest man on the face of the Earth. But of course, Lou Gehrig's statement was hyperbolic, and both lives shared the confluence of unspeakable tragedy with the blessings of extraordinary—but short—lives. Gehrig's teammate Sam Jones said that Lou was "the kind of person you'd like your son to be." Such a sentiment has been expressed about Clint, including by teammate Bob Kohl: "I hope my son Carson turns out to be the fun-loving, energetic, charismatic man that Clint embodied."

The life that my wife, Mary, and I loved sharing with Clint was cut short at its apex—within months after Clint's relocation to Charleston, South Carolina, to be closer to his parents as we approached the threshold of retirement years. He had recently begun with enthusiasm a new job with Merrill Lynch and had purchased his first home. Our loss came at a moment when our family of four had become energized with the prospects of our future decades together.

Like Lou Gehrig, Clint had lived a life abundant with joy, excitement, achievement, a loving family, and scores of dear friends. I know that during his life Clint considered himself to be "one of the luckiest men on the face of the Earth." And I know that Clint considered himself fortunate to be the son of parents who would provide him and Carly with opportunities to become just that.

"The afternoon that Clint and I played Kiawah's Ocean Course will forever live in my memory. With each good shot, Clint gained confidence and had that bounce in his step that made me proud. As we walked the course, we had time to reflect on many topics. As we walked up one fairway, he turned to me and said, 'I am so grateful for all of the things my father has done for me over the years. I know

so many guys who have not had the chance to experience what I have, and I owe it all to my dad.'"

—Clint's UNCLE CHUCK RUDEK

Clint and his uncle Chuck Rudek at Kiawah's Ocean Course

Clint's 2012 birthday message to me, still posted on his Facebook page, thanked me for being "the best father a son could have." After his tragic passing, I posted a Facebook message to him thanking *him* for being "the best son a parent could have." As with Lou Gehrig, Clint's future was limitless; his past, supremely rewarding.

I find comfort in knowing that hundreds of family members and friends understand the need to continue Clint's legacy. That legacy began moments after the declaration that his life on this Earth had ended, when his organs were donated to those in need, consistent with the wishes he had expressed months earlier when he applied for his South Carolina driver's license. I find comfort in the knowledge that Clint's heart has never stopped beating.

And while Clint's assailant could end his life, he could not end his dreams. They continue through the Clint Seymour "Play Ball" Fund, through which the joy of youth baseball will be enhanced, initially in greater Pittsburgh and Charleston. Its mission is to enable other children to experience the same positive impact that the game of baseball had on the development of Clint's character and personality, by providing young ball players with opportunities to enjoy the game while nurturing lasting character traits such as self-discipline, respect, determination, and self-esteem. The fund will celebrate the spirited joy of sprinting on and off the field, inhaling the special scent of a cowhide baseball, hearing the crack of the bat, and simply playing and recreating with friends old and new. After all, at its core, youth baseball is a form of "re-creation"—a new opportunity for imagination, discovery, and performance.

And Clint's legacy continues as his family and friends recognize the character traits that can be assimilated into their own lives for their benefit and the benefit of the lives of those they touch. Perhaps even a reader who did not know Clint can benefit from these reflections on his unforgettable twenty-seven-year life.

Clint and Don at EKU, fall 2004

TWO

In the Beginning

"He had a beautiful smile that immediately forced you to smile back, but his smile was also unique, because it told you he had something else to add—if you could just wait a second. His eyes sparkled and had a hint of mischief; you just knew they were looking for the next adventure."

—Jim Haak, coach and friend

The pink notepad phone message that I was handed said "Call home ASAP." My heart raced. Mary's maternity bag had been packed and ready. She had returned home earlier in the day from an uneventful doctor's appointment. But after I returned her call, I dashed to her side as fast as my blue Subaru would allow. Her hospital bag was already waiting in the driveway. She slid into the front seat. No conversation was necessary. By the time we reached the Fort Pitt Tunnel, it was peak rush hour, so I drove on the berm with signals flashing. I prayed silently that we would make it through the tunnel. The alternative was unthinkable. We made it through and then raced over to Magee-Womens Hospital.

We had been coached all about the procedures for registering at the hospital's front desk. Not that day. I scampered around to help Mary out of the car, then through the sliding front door, and straight into the women's restroom in the front hallway. From there, the hospital personnel immediately recognized that the birth of our first child was beginning. They wheeled Mary into the delivery room. A nearby hospital worker graciously removed and handed me his shoe covers, head cover, and gown. As I nervously stumbled into them, he guided me into the delivery room to be with my wife as our first child was born. Not exactly out of the playbook of the birthing classes that we had attended, but still the indescribably precious moment that new parents experience.

Mary and I had decided that we would name a male baby either Chris or Clint. Mary had assured me that we would know the right answer as soon as we saw our new baby. That was not as intuitive to me as it was to her, but I did not question the approach. Mary was right. Within minutes of his birth, we looked at our healthy new son and said in unison, "Hello, Clint."

I eventually walked back through that front door, and there was the blue Subaru still sitting there with its driver's side door wide open and the "ping ping ping" ringing as if to announce the arrival of Clint to the world. It was May 6, 1986, and it would be the last time he was early for anything.

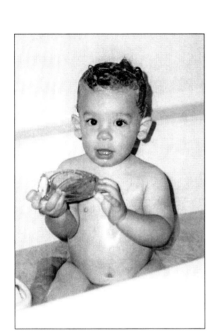

THREE

The Joy of the Game

"If I had to describe Clint in one word, it would be charismatic, because you would remember him for a lifetime after having just a single conversation with him."

—JERRY MAXCY, high school friend and teammate

Clint's first word was "ball." Even in his preschool years, there was nothing he enjoyed more than swinging a plastic baseball bat. He enjoyed even more those times when the bat would strike the ball and he would run instinctively . . . somewhere, anywhere.

At the age of five, his appetite for organized baseball was whetted when our friend Tom Birsic provided him an opportunity to serve as the batboy for a team he coached (with players barely older than Clint). Clint reacted with enthusiasm, and Tom's son Brian and his teammates warmly welcomed him to the team. Tom treated Clint as a young man, not as a five-year-old child, stressing to Clint that he had an important job to do, needed to arrive at the games on time, had to follow instructions, and could only drink one juice box after the games. Clint was hooked on baseball.

So when he reached the age of six, I searched for an opportunity to transfer his enthusiasm into a structure with

First swings at Osage Road

some adult supervision and instruction as well as opportunities to socialize with new friends. In our community of Mt. Lebanon in suburban Pittsburgh, the youth baseball program started at age eight. But I learned of a baseball program sponsored by the St. Louise de Marillac Catholic Church in neighboring Upper St. Clair that included seven-year-olds. I was a Protestant and Clint was only six, but the program sounded like a good fit for him. So I stretched the truth about Clint's age, agreed to work at their fish fry fundraisers, and learned that one of the leaders of the program was named Greenberg. So all seemed in order.

Clint's experience in the St. Louise program was the catalyst for the utter enjoyment that he felt for the rest of his life every time he stepped onto a baseball diamond. And, while I did not recognize it at the time, it would become the prototype for the influence that baseball would have upon the formation of Clint's personality and his character—his very essence.

The St. Louise program was guided by adults who were supportive of the seven-year-old players (and unknowingly one six-year-old as well). They maintained that delicate mix of encouraging the youngsters to learn the game—its rules and its skills—and to achieve success, while recognizing that the development of friendships and character traits even at that early age would remain with them long beyond their days on the diamond. Clint maintained friendships for the next two decades with a number of players he met in those few early seasons he played at St. Louise.

Clint had opportunities to play several seasons with a "traveling team" from St. Louise that would play in youth tournaments around greater Pittsburgh. The first year his team was coached by Craig Lee, the engaging son of a respected federal court judge and a perfect fit for youngsters wanting to enjoy their moments on the diamond with new friends. Clint quickly became friends with Coach Lee's sons, Conor and Sean, who each enjoyed their own subsequent athletic successes. Conor played soccer at the college level and later became the placekicker on Pitt's football team. Sean is now a starting linebacker for the Dallas Cowboys. Each has been as highly regarded off the field as on it. I expect that they both recognize the positive impact of those early St. Louise years. While youth experiences in team athletics can be important molding experiences, coaches and mentors must create an environment—as Craig Lee did—in which the young players enjoy the experience in order to reap its rewards. Clint enjoyed sprinting on and off the field every game and every practice at St. Louise.

In his last year or two at St. Louise, Clint came under the coaching tutelage of Chuck Greenberg, who managed a successful travel team from St. Louise. Those were the "coach pitch" years, and I would soon recognize that the key to success was the ability of the coach to throw hittable pitches to his players. Chuck was a master of the craft, and he is left-handed, permitting his mostly right-handed batters to see the ball a bit longer. Chuck was assisted by some other parent coaches, including Jack McGraw and former Pitt basketball star Tom Richards. They had a touch for balancing the determination to succeed with other values, not the least of which was developing friendships in those formative years with other youth who shared similar values, and simply enjoying every moment on the field and the accompanying socialization, on and off the diamond. One season that St. Louise travel team finished with a perfect 17–0 record. The eight-year-old players (and one seven-year-old) were ecstatic with their record and with the fun they had in collectively achieving it. The team rode around the St. Louise parking lot in my dad's antique Model A convertible in celebration. The players, keying off their coaches, were supportive of each other. They were respectful of opponents and umpires and the game itself. At the conclusion of the season, Chuck Greenberg addressed his players:

> *"You guys just accomplished something that was awesome. You finished our season unbeaten. Someday you will understand how unusual that is and how difficult it is to achieve that. You may never again play on an undefeated team. So be proud of what you as a team have accomplished and of how you accomplished it."*

The parents understood what Chuck was saying. The players *heard* what Chuck was saying, and I am sure that over the ensuing years, they also *understood* what he was saying. (Chuck, by the way, would become CEO of the Texas Rangers in 2010.)

During those years, Clint was introduced to Matt Bianco, a former Pitt baseball star, who upon graduation had set up a modest "baseball school" in what had been an empty storefront in a shopping strip near our home. Clint was one of

Undefeated St. Louise team, circa 1993

Matt's first and youngest students. Clint was being introduced to baseball as a six-year-old, while Matt was learning
how to teach it. The two novices would both succeed. Each
time Clint arrived at the tiny storefront for his time with
Matt, I couldn't tell whose smile was brighter. But I could
tell that my son was developing an association between
baseball and fun that never ceased.

Clint later followed Matt into a larger facility he developed farther out in the suburbs. Eventually Clint also trained
there under the tutelage of Frank Merigliano for pitching
instruction as Clint's baseball path developed. Matt and
Frank each have their own baseball academies now. Each
had a keen understanding that they were instructing Clint
on lessons much broader than his baseball skills. Clint never
required coaxing to attend any of his scheduled "lessons"
with Matt or Frank.

The same can be said with gusto for his experiences with
Al Liberi, who provided more advanced batting instruction
for Clint in his high school and college years. Al had a tiny,

eclectic storefront facility in Carnegie within the shadow of Honus Wagner's birthplace. There was just enough room for one batting cage. But that cage, a bucket of balls, and a three-legged stool was all he needed. And that's all he had— plus an aging eight-track tape player that cycled Frank Sinatra throughout the hours. Al was a character. Clint found him intriguing. Al possessed a rare gift for analyzing a baseball swing and fine-tuning it, but his greatest influence was the boundless energy and enthusiasm that he infused into his baseball students. While he had no formal training in the behavioral sciences, Al's aptitude at building confidence in his pupils would be a model template for any coach or mentor of youth. He had been around baseball long enough to understand that a player's confidence was as vital to success as his physical skills. Anyone who spent time with Al would be enriched by that life lesson.

With Carly and Nonny (Hazel "Dixie" Seymour) and Poppy (Robert E. Seymour)

The joy of the postgame snack

FOUR

The Allure of the Game

"Looking back, I don't know how anyone kept up with Clint. There was an energy about him that was contagious, and everyone gravitated toward it. He also had a warm soul if you ever were lucky enough to have a one-on-one conversation with him. Don, you should be extremely proud of your son for always bringing a smile and laugh to everyone he met. I'm honored to call Clint my friend."

—DREW ISLER, friend and Mt. Lebanon teammate

MT. LEBANON BASEBALL

The core of Clint's baseball experience was rooted in Mt. Lebanon, where he played in programs sponsored by the community's youth baseball association from ages eight through fourteen (1994 through 2000) and where he played high school varsity baseball for four years (2001 through 2004). He was a first-team all-state selection as an outfielder his senior year and is included in the high school's sports hall of champions.

Starting at age eight, when Clint played in the community's baseball program, he and his fellow players were ably led by a board headed by Dan Bowman, Scott Isler, and George Jackson. I would occasionally coach a team, but it did not take me long to learn that others were better suited and that coaching my son's team was definitely a mixed bag.

I was coaching a team of eight-year-olds in a routine game in the dust of Markham School field one summer evening when I noticed our left fielder depart from the field in a hurry. I had become accustomed to hasty exit if a youngster had consumed his water bottle too quickly and needed relief behind a nearby tree. And at that age, the left fielder was not always intensely engaged in the contest anyway. But the boy kept running, past several suitable sycamores, and I was becoming concerned. Soon I saw him scamper into an arriving automobile that I could only hope was not driven by a registered sex offender. I launched into my version of a sprint across the dust toward the parking lot before realizing that there was no way I would arrive in time to assure that I had not just witnessed the abduction of one of my eight-year-old players.

His remaining teammates, finding glee in my dilemma, hailed me back to the bench to reassure me that the outfielder was merely addicted to the *Teenage Mutant Ninja Turtles* cartoon show, which was televised daily at 7:30 p.m. Apparently, the treaty that the youngster had negotiated with his mother was that he would attend the scheduled games only on the condition that he could be released from service promptly at 7:20 p.m. (as long as he could take an early dip into the postgame juice box cooler before his departure). Clint and I chuckled over that one for years, with Clint's repetition of the events becoming increasingly embellished and decreasingly charitable toward the unwitting coach as the years passed.

Those early years were a blast and were great fun for the kids. For many, it was their first exposure to a team sport and the many disciplines of learning the rules of the game, obeying the restrictions imposed for their safety, understanding how to be responsible for and to care for their own equipment, and being on time for practices and games. The majority of the youngsters would not play organized baseball beyond age twelve, but there was nothing better for the families in our community than an hour or two on a lawn chair under some wispy clouds on a summer evening with new friends, no pressure to perform, an assured juice box and hug after the final out, and maybe even a pizza at Mineo's. We all learned the healthiest seven words, according to leadership expert Tim Elmore, that parents can offer a child at that age before a game: *Have fun. Play hard. I love you.*

After a several-year hiatus from coaching, when Clint was eleven, I succumbed to the temptation and agreed to coach a team comprised of eleven- and twelve-year-olds. When the coaches gathered in the metaphorical smoke-filled room to draft the players for the teams, I had the distinct disadvantage of not knowing the twelve-year-old players, and drafting a twelve-year-old pitcher was regarded as a priority. When it came time for my first-round selection, I asked the assembled intelligentsia which twelve-year-old pitchers remained. Apparently, there was only one left (Jerry), but I knew some good eleven-year-old pitchers. However, the consensus recommendation was that I should select a twelve-year-old. Since I did not know Jerry, I went through my due diligence.

"Does Jerry throw hard?"

"Oh yes."

"Will Jerry walk a ton of batters?"

"Oh no."

"Well behaved?"

"Oh yes."

"Well, then Jerry is my pick."

Only then was it revealed that "Gerri" (not Jerry) was Geraldine, and a few of the seasoned, gnarled veterans could not suppress a snicker. Well, it turned out that Gerri was a gem and a joy (or was she a jem and a goy?). She was a very capable pitcher, an even better shortstop, and an accomplished hitter, as well as being a wonderful teammate and a natural leader for the eleven-year-olds. In retrospect, she would have been my top choice in the draft had I held its first pick. A seasoned, gnarled veteran probably won the league that year, but Gerri and I and the rest of our team did just fine.

I didn't coach during Clint's twelve-year-old season. Clint's team and his good friend Andy Goff's team were rivals for the league championship. Andy and Clint had played together on the Mt. Lebanon travel team since they were eight and had become good friends. Andy's father, Dan, had coached the travel team most of those years, and the Goff and Seymour families had become friends, appreciating each other's sons' accomplishments as teammates and occasionally as rivals in the Mt. Lebanon intra-community league. Predictably, their two teams advanced to the championship game at Mt. Lebanon's Dixon Field in 1998. I happened to be working in Boston that day, disappointed to be missing the game. When I awoke the next morning to the realization that *The Boston Globe* did not carry the box score, I called home to learn that Clint had hit a home run off Andy (which was a rare occurrence) that contributed to a victory in a close game. It would be the last game that they played against each other, although hundreds of games as teammates on four different teams lay ahead for Clint and Andy.

Players who were interested in challenging themselves and learning how to play the game at a more competitive level had opportunities to play for one of the several travel teams at each age level that played a summer season of tournaments around Western Pennsylvania. At Clint's age group, the adult energy behind those Mt. Lebanon travel teams was Dan Goff (with a big assist from Bob Bannon in the early years). Dan surrounded himself with other parents who could nominally serve as assistants, but he had that ideal combination of enormous athletic ability and an enormous heart.

Each year, that Mt. Lebanon travel team had notable success among its Western Pennsylvania competitors, developing steadily from age eight through age twelve. Clint again was blessed to be surrounded by a dozen players of high character and special athletic ability. Over its five seasons, the players on that team responded well to Dan's encouragement to achieve personal and team goals while being exposed to the synergies that arise naturally from association with contemporaries of high character in those formative years. I still have not figured out whether high character induces high achievement or vice versa, but Clint's baseball experiences convinced me of the interrelationship. The core players on that travel team over the years included Clint, Andy, Steve Basheda, Scott Brown, Ed Contestible, Marty Dattilo, Eric Drobotij, Ryan Eckenrode, Jeff Elias, Matt Franchick, Drew Isler, Pat Kerr, Bill Leckenby, David Tickle, and Andy Zych. Clint kept in touch with all of them, with social media providing valuable conduits for those geographically distant. They have each matured into the young men that their formative years in baseball would have projected.

Every baseball team—even in the major leagues—has a coach who is informally regarded as the "players' coach," someone who is always approachable and insulated a bit from the head coach. On the Mt. Lebanon travel teams, Phil Kerr was the natural. At one point Phil encountered a health issue that had the players concerned. Although his son Pat continued to play, Phil was confined to hospital rooms and bed rest at home for a number of games. As the team was preparing for an important tournament game at Upper St. Clair and departing the field from their pregame drills, Phil (led by the hand of his wife, Carol) was spotted slowly and carefully approaching a viewing perch atop a steep slope behind the first-base bench. No one had to say a word. Andy started and all the rest followed, climbing that steep hill to give Phil a hug and a pledge that they would win the game for him. They did. Phil would tell you they were winners that day before the game even started.

As that travel team flourished, the followers of Mt. Lebanon High School baseball began to whisper. When that class of 2004 got to high school, joining the class of 2002's two premier left-handed pitchers (Chris Koutsavlis and Adam Snyder) and some talented position players, such as infielders Steve Maiolo and Justin Steranka, outfielder Brad Russell, and catcher Matt DiGiovanni, many thought that the upcoming teams could rival the 1998 state champion team. The 1998 Blue Devils had been very special, sending a number of graduates into college baseball programs and producing two players who remain in the major leagues. Josh Wilson, the team's shortstop, is now with the Texas Rangers, and Don Kelly, the team's second baseman, is now with the Detroit Tigers. In fact, each of those alumni has had notable careers. Josh has changed teams eleven times, and Don is the only active MLB player (and one of only five in history) to have played every one of the nine positions in at least one major league game. That 1998 team was coached by the legendary Ed McCloskey and was blessed with a number of talented players in addition to Josh and Don. Clint and Andy were inspired by watching their games on a quasi-baseball field behind Mellon Junior High School. They were impressed and inspired when Josh and Don were each drafted into professional baseball.

Clint with Don Kelly at Neil and Niki Walker's
wedding

In 2001, both Clint and Andy made the varsity roster of the high school team as freshmen, Andy as the starting second baseman and Clint as a reserve outfielder. Mark Saghy, who had been Ed McCloskey's assistant, had become the head coach upon Ed's retirement. Ed's son, Patt, became Mark's assistant. It was as capable and devoted a coaching combination as existed in Western Pennsylvania. Clint loved playing for both of them. They each epitomized the best of coaching and were loyal to and supportive of their players. Mark was a bastion of stability, always in control of the game. He enjoyed an excellent reputation among other coaches and players. There is no doubt he had high aspirations, particularly for the upcoming 2002–2004 teams.

Mark's assistant, Patt McCloskey, was also special to Clint. He was a teacher in the social sciences department at the high school and taught Clint for two years. Clint had high regard for him as a teacher and was in awe of his intellect. But what really impressed Clint was an apocryphal story about Patt when he played high school baseball at Mt. Lebanon. Legend had it that, after a defeat at the hands of archrival North Allegheny in the playoffs one year, Patt was so determined to start preparation for the following season and avenge that defeat that he departed the team bus and went directly to the Cedar Boulevard batting cages and started hitting off a batting tee under the light of the moon, which soon disappeared as rain swept in. The harder it rained, the harder Patt swung, until his batting gloves and then his bare hands were ravaged. Clint absolutely loved repeating that story, which he described as "epic." As with the stories that he enjoyed telling about his father, this one had that perfect confluence of hyperbolic humor and an underlying admiration for its subject.

Any high school student would be fortunate to be taught by Patt McCloskey and to play for Mark or Patt. Patt is now the head coach of the Mt. Lebanon High School team, and when the team won the section championship this year (2014), it dedicated the clinching game to Clint.

"Our entire program is deeply saddened beyond words," Patt told the media. "I had the privilege to coach him for four years and taught him for two years. He was the nicest and most fun-loving kid. He was the epitome of life and baseball in Mt. Lebanon."

By the time Clint's class worked its way onto the high school team, a number of its core players had diverted their athletic attention to other sports. Soccer, lacrosse, and hockey had gained steadily in popularity and had attracted formidable baseball talent like Pat Kerr, Matt Franchick, Bill Leckenby, Ed Contestible, and Marty Dattilo. But Andy (who was also the football quarterback) and Clint stayed with baseball and, after their freshman seasons on the varsity team, were joined by classmates Scott Brown, Eric Drobotij, Tyler Vallano, Jeff Elias, Drew Isler, Ryan Eckenrode, Jack Millhouse, Dan Torcasi, Jeff Myers, and others as a strong nucleus from that class infusing itself into the high school team. In

2002 (Clint's sophomore year), the team won the coveted Western Pennsylvania (WPIAL) championship. The WPIAL was what it was all about. High school baseball followers in the region were much more aware of the WPIAL champions (which was where the bragging rights rested) than the state champions. The 2002 Mt. Lebanon team was highly success-ful, at one point being ranked as high as sixteenth in the nation by *USA Today*. That 2002 WPIAL championship game was memorable. Pitcher Chris Koutsavlis capped a re-markable season with a no-hitter, besting Blackhawk's Brian Omogrosso, who would go on to pitch in the major leagues for the White Sox. Andy and Clint were both starters. Clint contributed a hit, a run, and a nifty outfield catch in the 2–0 win. The team, coaches, and parents celebrated with pizza upstairs at Bado's on Beverly Road. And when that concluded, Harry Snyder (Adam's father) and I wandered into the all-night Eat'n Park for coffee, not wanting the night to end.

The 2004 season was successful by most standards, but Clint, Andy, and the other seniors had hoped to emulate the successes of the 1998 and 2002 championship teams.

Mt. Lebanon High School 2002 WPIAL champions (Mark Sagby, coach)

At the Weirton, WV tournament

With the "Hardware"

Mt. Lebanon High School, 2004

*Mt. Lebanon vs. North Allegheny
2002, post-season*

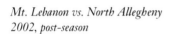

*After the inaugural WPIAL
All-Star game, 2004*

The 2004 team won its section, but hit a bump in the road against a good Latrobe team whose pitcher Tim Flynn threw nothing but curveballs to a Blue Devil batting order that had mastered most pitchers that season. But, as the adage goes, "good pitching will defeat good hitting." (Leave it to Yogi Berra to say, "Good pitching beats good hitting or vice versa.") Mt. Lebanon's pitcher Tyler Vallano, with late inning relief from Eric Drobotij, pitched the game of his life, certainly good enough to win most days. But the Latrobe hurler was exceptional in throwing a one-hitter, placing curveball after curveball in good locations in a performance rarely witnessed at the high school level. Clint put a good swing on one in the first inning that I thought had a chance, but it was caught by the center fielder at the fence, and that was as close as the team would come to scoring a run in the heartbreaking 1–0 loss. It would be a melancholy closing to Clint's high school baseball experience. But for Clint, Andy, Eric, and Tyler, college baseball awaited them.

"I know that I will smile as I tell my children someday about my amazing and funny friend Clint who wore a zany suit from the Goodwill to our high school dance."

—Rebecca Gunn, friend

Steel City Wildcats

When Clint and his classmates were twelve years old (the 1998 baseball season), I shared with some other coaches who I had come to know from other Western Pennsylvania programs my sense that Little League-sized baseball diamonds had become inappropriate for twelve-year-old players. The more advanced twelve-year-old pitchers were throwing sixty miles per hour from forty-five feet. An eleven-year-old batter who was not highly skilled was at risk. And modern-day twelve-year-olds had outgrown the sixty-foot base paths. The game had progressed over the years, with the advent of metal bats and youngsters who were becoming bigger and stronger, but the dimensions had not adjusted. I hypothesized that we could assemble a team of twelve-year-olds from around the region to play at larger-scaled fields that they would not see in Western Pennsylvania until they were older. I shared my thought originally with Dan Goff and with Jamie Abercrombie (Sr.) and Tom Walker of Brad-Mar-Pine in the North Hills. They warmed to the concept immediately, and from their perspectives the prospect of playing baseball at a more competitive level for interested players was also intriguing.

We acknowledged a couple of basics. First, if we could assemble such a team, we would need to travel to other regions of the country where twelve-year-olds were already playing at larger-scaled fields, which would require an uncommon commitment from twelve-year-olds and their parents. And second, we would not interfere with the programs of the local baseball associations that were the lifeblood of youth baseball in Western Pennsylvania. So the game plan was to travel to select locations (which eventually extended from Ontario to Florida and from Eastern Pennsylvania to Indiana) on schedules that did not interfere with local associations' programs (that had a limited duration in any event because of weather conditions in the North). The plan was starting to crystallize. There was, however, one additional challenge. We had no field. Not a problem. We would practice where we traveled as much as we could, and we would play only "away" games. The seed quickly germinated, and the Steel City Wildcats team was born. We decided to practice in the winters with whoever could attend at Bianco's or in an abandoned steel mill–cum–baseball facility in Bridgeville.

We managed to keep the team together for four years (with modest roster variations from year to year as a few players and families understandably realized that the commitment was burdensome and because we needed more pure pitchers for games condensed into a weekend). There had not been a team in Western Pennsylvania with this template for as long as anyone could remember (although my friends Tom Birsic and Joe Duff had fielded teams with some similarities that I shamelessly plagiarized).

> *"The time we shared with the boys during those years was the most rewarding and enjoyable period of my life, and Clint was a major reason for that. I think of those times often and never without smiling, nodding, and knowing we did something we could all be proud of."*
>
> —JIM HAAK, coach and friend

My "baseball goal" for our players was to prepare them to play high school baseball. We succeeded beyond my aspirations. All of our guys played high school baseball successfully. In fact, if you looked at the dozen or so players who were the core of the team over our four-year existence, ten played college baseball (Clint at Eastern Kentucky, Andy at Wake Forest, Jim Gallagher at Duke, Dale Mollenhauer at East Carolina, Bill Torre at Duquesne, Mike Schmidt at West Virginia, Jamie Abercrombie Jr. at Temple, Jason Mesko at Point Park, and Eric Drobotij at Mercyhurst, plus Neil Walker, who had committed to Clemson before the Pittsburgh Pirates signed him as their first-round draft pick in 2004). And Jim (White Sox), Dale (White Sox and Orioles), Andy (Rockies), and Neil (Pirates) played professional baseball. Neil, as the Pirates' second baseman, has become one of the best in baseball, winning a 2014 Silver Slugger Award.

On the diamond, the team started out respectably and eventually improved to become recognized for its achievement and its class. I told the team that the most important statistic I tracked was that we were batting 100 percent in the number of teams we played in a weekend series who invited us back. There was nothing subtle about my reminder that—without a home field—being gracious visitors was a priority. Our 100 percent record in that regard validated everything that we had set out to accomplish.

We once traveled to Greenfield, Indiana, the home of poet James Whitcomb Riley, a literary footnote that I announced without generating an animated response from the squad. We played a select team from the area that had a unique model, having purchased a corn field adjacent to Interstate 70, constructed a self-storage complex, and used its revenue to construct and maintain a small but elegant baseball complex. It became apparent that we had more talent than our host team was able to field. When a score got a bit lopsided, we would always play "one base at a time" ball. Our hosts knew and appreciated what was happening, and they recognized a team that could be gracious in victory. As we were packing to return to Pennsylvania, their coach approached me and thanked me for the valuable experience his team gained from the weekend—exposure to a team that played the game like we did and that respected their opponents, the umpires, and the game itself. Of course, a team led by coaches Bob Mollenhauer, Jim Haak, Dan Goff, Tom Walker, and Jamie Abercrombie would be capable of nothing less. The Indiana coach then invited us to return the next season as their guests for the season's opening weekend kickoff celebration of games. When we returned, our guys were treated like rock stars with a huge barbeque picnic. And the games were a little closer.

On the field, we made amazing progress over the seasons. We won many of the tournaments we entered, including the prestigious "Beast of the East" in Wheeling, West Virginia, that attracted teams from all over the eastern United States. In 2000, we played in the AAU 14U national tournament in Sarasota, Florida. With representatives from coast to coast forming a field of sixty-eight teams, we made it to the trophy round and finished sixth, the highest finish of any northern team. We were knocked out by the Dallas team, which was coached by Cecil Espy, a former Pittsburgh Pirate and a class act. The following year we qualified for the AAU nationals again, this time in Kingsport, Tennessee. It rained constantly, so we played through some bad weather and soggy fields. We did not make it to the trophy round this time, but we played respectably in what would be our last tournament appearance. The players were on their high school teams by then, and we had more than fulfilled the goal of preparing them for a successful experience at that level.

I am told by some players who kept track of these things that we won more than 80 percent of our games against the best competition we could find. Suffice it to say, on the diamond, this team was "legit."

My non-baseball goal for our players was to make new friends from around Western Pennsylvania who had been selected for their character, as well as their playing ability. While we succeeded with my baseball goal, we hit a grand slam with my non-baseball goal. The enjoyment that these players experienced and the lessons they learned (mostly from each other) were indescribable.

The teammates remain friends. Social media and SoHo (see Chapter Nine) helped, as these young people developed friendships and respect for each other that they valued and reinforced every time they were together. Two of them delivered eulogies (see Epilogue) with eyes swollen for a friend who hadn't been a teammate for a dozen years. I comforted three young men at the Pittsburgh memorial service with the message that while parents should never face burying a child, it follows that young men their age should never face eulogizing a friend. They spoke with conviction about their friend and their cousin to a riveted audience—an audience that was witnessing not only tributes to Clint but also the demonstration of the transformation into maturity that metaphorically mirrored Clint himself at age twenty-seven. It was no accident.

I know that Bob Kohl spoke for all of his Steel City teammates when he sent me this message:

"Don, I'm writing you this email because I want to be like you when I grow up. I hope my son, Carson, turns out to be the fun-loving, energetic, charismatic man that Clint embodied. It was truly a blessing to have spent the years of my life around you and Clint, when young men are the most easily influenced and guidance is a key component. . . . At an early age you took a bunch of kids from Pittsburgh before AAU ball was even talked about there, and gave all of us a chance to better ourselves through competition and creating a family atmosphere in everything we did. My dad thought the world of you and your generosity, and I now [as a parent] know why. . . . Clint was a great ball player and friend of mine during those days. That's what I will always remember him for . . . one hell of a dude. Fun was what we had; the ball-playing was a by-product."

Bob was spot on. Fun was what we all had, that's for sure.

"I loved to watch Clint hit. But my favorite memories of Clint were not on the ball field. Clint would never pass up an adventure, and white-water rafting certainly qualified. Showing up with white garden gloves and goggles didn't help much on the river but definitely added to the legend. The fact that Don informed me, as we were loading the van, that Clint wasn't much for swimming—but to do the best you can—further enhanced it. The trip went off like clockwork, with Clint and me thrown out on the same rapid. . . . Of the dozens of trips we took and hundreds of games we played, Clint and I spoke about the rafting trip, running on the field at the "Big House" at Ann Arbor, the buffet in South Carolina, and the many other soirees we shared far more than any baseball memory. That Clint and I maintained a relationship past the Steel City Wildcats is a testament to the value of our time together."

—Jim Haak, coach and friend

Bill Torre, another teammate of Clint's for all of our seasons, who went on to play for Mike Wilson at Duquesne University, explained some of the value he derived from his Steel City experience with Clint:

"Over the past week, I have shared stories with friends and family, people who have never met Clint. . . . I explained Clint's personality, his kindness, and how he put so much passion into everything that he did. Please know that Clint's spirit and legacy will live on through my life. My girlfriend has learned of Clint, my kids will learn of Clint, and I will live my life with more zest and excitement as Clint taught us all how to do."

Our team achieved some notoriety and media attention in Pittsburgh, causing many people to ask me for the for-

Clint with coach/friend Jim Haak

mula for what we had accomplished. It can be expressed more simply than it can be attained. Assemble youth at that age into a group activity (whether it is baseball or the marching band or Eagle Scouts) with others of high character, led by adults who are the role models we all want our children to emulate, and the players will figure out the rest of it themselves. It was magical to see how positively our team members reacted to subtle influences from their peers and teammates if their behavior patterns (or their baseball performance) needed recalibration. And how much joy they found when the adults were at an appropriate distance.

> *"The team was playing in the AAU national tournament in Florida, and all the adults went out for dinner and left the players back at the hotel for pizza. When we came back, we saw they all had shrimp cocktail that Clint had charged to Don's room."*
>
> —LUANNE HAAK, friend

Andy Goff and Clint between games at 2000 14U AAU national championship tournament, Sarasota, Florida

Steel City Wildcats at Neil and Niki Walker's wedding included Tom Walker (coach), Tyler Haak, Clint Seymour, Jim Haak (coach), Jim Gallagher, Dale Mollenhauer, Don Seymour (coach), Jamie Abercrombie, and Neil Walker

AAU National Tournament 2000 (14U): (front) Jim Gallagher, Jim Ellis, Ty Haak, Dale Mollenhauer, Bill Torre, (back) Coach Bob Mollenhauer, Coach Jim Haak, Andy Goff, Eric Drobotij, Neil Walker, Coach Dan Goff, Clint Seymour, Brad Devett, Coach Don Seymour

AAU National Tournament 2001 (15U): (front)Jim Gallagher, Ty Haak, Bill Torre, Scott Brown, Dale Mollenhauer, Clint Seymour, (back) Coach Bob Mollenhauer, Coach Jim Haak, Bob Kohl, Mike Schmidt, Neil Walker, Andy Goff, Jason Mesko, Eric Drobotij, Coach Don Seymour

THAT'S WHAT FRIENDS ARE FOR

"Clint was like a brother to me."

—NEIL WALKER, friend and teammate

Clint and Neil at Bradenton's McKechnie Field, February 2014

One of the early defining moments of our first Steel City season came in Buffalo, New York, where Neil Walker, our twelve-year-old catcher who was learning to switch-hit, belted homers from each side in the same game. That was, for me, a revelation that Neil was an exceptional talent, as well as being a special young man and one of the natural leaders on the team.

After four seasons with the Steel City Wildcats, Neil progressed through Pine Richland High School to a berth on the USA Baseball seventeen-year-old team, eventually committing to a scholarship to play baseball at Clemson. When the Pittsburgh Pirates made him their first-round pick of the 2004 draft, he predictably chose a professional baseball career. Eventually, the Pirates converted him from a catcher to an infielder. He has been a mainstay as the Pirates' second baseman since 2010. Through it all, he remained friends with his Steel City Wildcats teammates, including Clint, Ty Haak, Dale Mollenhauer, Jim Gallagher, Jamie Abercombie, Andy Goff, and others. He could spend time with these friends and rely upon their bedrock friendships to normalize and stabilize his life in the public eye, as a refuge, where he could play golf or fish or play cards in the relaxed, unpretentious company of guys who knew him as an old friend, not as a major league ballplayer.

Neil and his wife, Niki, and Clint (and Tyler if he was in town) would sit at our kitchen table in South Carolina on their way to Bradenton, Florida, where the Pirates hold spring training, and play cards every evening of their stay until the wee hours, never tiring of each other's company or wit. The game they played has a name that most major league baseball players would recognize, but this book would lose its G rating if repeated. It seemed to have no rules except that at some point a player would make a seemingly arbitrary, exuberant declaration of victory. If Ty was not at the table, I might be asked to join, with wry grins from Clint and Neil and Niki, who knew what was about to occur. It did not matter that I did not know the rules, because it did not seem that there were any. Tiring of my predictable plight, I would sometimes simply just declare victory for the hand—just as exuberantly as the others—but with no impact other than a bogus explanation of why I hadn't just won. The game seemed to flow smoothly with a foil at the table.

Just weeks after Clint's last card game and pizza-making contest at the Walkers' home in Bradenton, I had to send Neil a text I never could have imagined. He read the text in the visitors' clubhouse at Busch Stadium in St. Louis follow-

Neil and Niki Walker at one of the marathon card games

ing that Saturday night's Pirates game against the Cardinals.

After speaking with Neil, Colin Dunlap, a talented Pittsburgh sports journalist, wrote a respectful and sensitive article about what happened next, published on the Pittsburgh CBS radio website on May 6, 2014 (pittsburgh.cbslocal.com):

> . . . Walker pushed through the rest of that St. Louis [Saturday] night, trying as much as he could to determine what had happened. . . .
>
> How were Seymour's parents going to deal with this moving forward?
>
> How was Walker, himself, going to deal with this moving forward?
>
> And then, after a restless night, Walker had to take the field for the Pirates in that Sunday game.
>
> "That was the first time in my entire life that my mind was anywhere but the baseball field while I was on it," Walker said. "As creatures of habit in baseball, you're always able to get into a mode and just focus on

the game. That day, I couldn't. . . ."

For Walker, as he recalled the life of his friend, it had nothing to do with how it prematurely ended, instead, the experiences the two realized together.

Walker and Seymour started playing together . . . when their fathers were part of a group that formed the Steel City Wildcats. . . .

"We didn't really have a home field," Walker said. "We traveled a lot, so you grew close. Clint and I hit it off and he loved baseball as much as I did. He was the kind of friend you wanted to surround yourself with."

So much so that as Walker's journey negotiated through the minor leagues and then back to his beloved Pittsburgh—and Seymour's through college baseball and jobs in Pittsburgh and then South Carolina—the two remained close, taking every opportunity they could to get together. . . .

"He was definitely a special person, special to me and special to a lot of people," Walker said. "This has all kind of made me realize more to appreciate each day, to have fun with what you're doing, to make sure to appreciate all you have and how appreciative I am to play this game for a living.

"And how grateful I am to have known Clint."

Neil told Bobby Kerlick of the Pittsburgh *Tribune-Review* in an April 29, 2014, article:

"Clint was a dear, special friend to me and my wife. His heart and charisma lifted so many people that he met over the years. He always had a smile on his face and knew how to make everyone around him smile. He will be missed greatly, but we will always cherish the special memories we had with him while he was on this earth."

Neil spoke further of his twenty-year friendship with Clint during his eulogy at the May 12, 2014, Pittsburgh memorial service:

> *"In my profession, there is a certain level of player that exudes extreme confidence in everything that he does. Clint Seymour was one of those people. He lived his life without regret and as if he didn't care who was watching. . . . He played every pitch and inning as if it could be his last. . . . Everything he did was with conviction, tireless effort, confidence, and a goal to be the absolute best he could be.*
>
> *Clint made me a better person, on the baseball field, where we pushed each other to be the best, and off the field. Everything he was involved in he wanted to be the best at—running, fishing, golfing, bartending, caddying, sales, or being a financial advisor; and that tireless effort flowed into the people who surrounded him to push themselves to be the best they could be."*

On April 28, Neil and Niki rushed to Charleston to be

Neil Walker, Pirates second baseman

with Clint, arriving on the first plane from Baltimore that Monday morning to say goodbye to their friend, even though I had forewarned them that he would be nonresponsive. It was fitting that when the inevitable, wrenching declaration was made by the doctors that afternoon, Neil and Niki were with Clint, Mary, Carly, and me.

From my perspective, Neil's baseball stats will always pale in comparison to the good times that Clint had with Neil and Niki over the years that had nothing to do with baseball. I will continue to watch the box scores every day, but what I will remember most is Neil and Niki holding my son's hand, kissing his cheek, and whispering in his ear.

That's what friends are for.

Neil and Clint after the inaugural WPIAL All-Star game, 2004

Clint and Neil at Bradenton

Clint, Ty, Neil, Niki, with Elvis and Lucky Seymour and Oliver Walker at Seabrook Island

FIVE

National Championships

"Don: I am proud to say that Clint was one of my favorite guys on that [2003 BP] team and one that I will never forget. He indeed did make everyone around him feel comfortable and somehow found a way to brighten up the room. I am honored to have known him. My little brother was a batboy on the team that year, and Clint was all he talked about. All day. "Hey Adam, will Clint be at the next game?" He made an impact on a lot of people that you're probably unaware of. I won't ever forget the way he welcomed me to the team and kept me calm when things weren't going the way I wanted them to. Thank you for allowing your son to play a role in a part of my life."

—ADAM DIMICHELE, friend and BP teammate and former quarterback, Temple University and Philadelphia Eagles

T he Western Pennsylvania towns hugging the valleys of Pittsburgh's fabled three rivers historically produced most of the steel in the region and many of its notable athletes—Honus Wagner, Stan Musial, Dick Groat, Ken Griffey, Joe Namath, Johnny Unitas, Tony Dorsett, and Mike Ditka among them. As the steel industry declined and the population moved more to suburban communities from the mill towns along the rivers, the athletic notables predictably were found increasingly in the growing suburbs.

Clint and Andy after their last game as teammates

Mike Kosko was the product of a mill town where, at any time of the day or night, the furnaces and slag dumps lit up its skies and young Mike could be found on its streets. Summoning all the grit of that environment, and motivated to escape it, Mike was able to work his way into college and eventually to employment at West Mifflin High School, overlooking the deserted furnaces of the U.S. Steel Works at Homestead and Duquesne. His devotion to baseball landed him the head baseball coaching position at West Mifflin High School and later an indoor batting facility called BP (short for "batting practice"), where Mike supplemented his income giving baseball lessons and where many committed high school players used the cages regularly in the off-season.

Baseball was in his blood. Even after leaving the West Mifflin coaching position, he was determined to assemble a handpicked team of high school juniors and seniors and offer them the best baseball experience in the region, preparing them for baseball at the college level (a level at which he had once coached at Penn State McKeesport, now Penn State Greater Allegheny). His team (variously known as BP or the Bulldogs) presented an opportunity for some of the region's more prominent players to achieve visibility to college coaches through Mike's networking, through showcases he held, and through tournaments to which the team traveled. He found most (but not all) of the players from the suburban communities, not the streets of the mill towns that had forged his character. Mike was cognizant of what he regarded as an incongruity of the upbringing he had on the streets of the mill towns with that of most of his players. It caused him to drive his players hard, and challenge them in ways he thought they might not have been challenged before. The players sensed that. They responded with redoubled effort.

Mike Kosko was made for this type of team. Younger players would have required a lighter touch than the seventeen- and eighteen-year-olds he assembled. They regarded him with respect even though he did not seem to be much older than they were. And he had moments when his emotions would go over the top. As he told a local sports reporter, "I yell and scream, but that is my philosophy. Some don't like it, but that's what I do. If you look past that, my whole goal is to make them the best they can be."

Clint told me once that it was not difficult to play for Coach Kosko, even though there were times that his on-field behavior could have made parents of little leaguers squirm. "We all know what to listen to and what not to listen to, and what we listen to is worth listening to." There you had it. A players' coach, who was steadfastly loyal to his players, like the children he didn't (yet) have. He was demanding, but these kids were seventeen and eighteen and intent on continuing their baseball careers. Mike recognized that at that age, these players needed to be led by an independent and experienced coach, not their prior parent-coaches. He was right. And there was nothing in this for Mike personally other than perpetuating his love of the game. He drove long distances to games and tournaments in a car seemingly in constant need of repair. He scoured the hills and valleys of Western Pennsylvania for high school players willing to chase achievable dreams and mature enough to endure exposure to an occasional rant.

The rewards for fusing all of that energy into his caldron were the ingots of two consecutive national championships. The first was the NABF (National Amateur Baseball Federation) 18U championship at London, Ontario, in 2003, and the second was a repeat of that national championship in Jackson, Mississippi, the following year. (The NABF championship is believed to be the oldest national amateur baseball championship in the world.) Mike was a bit of an enigma to the players—not the most organized coach and sometimes a little hard to follow. But there was no doubt that he was a good, solid baseball guy, and his players learned much from him at a time when they needed that knowledge to prepare them for college or professional baseball. They were his life. A guy with an edge forged by his early years on the streets, proud that some of that edge might be absorbed by a player who had not experienced it before.

Clint loved playing for him. He was just as off-center as Clint was, and Clint quickly sized up when to take Mike's rants seriously and when to stoically ignore them. Mike's players knew he was always there for them. And the experience for players like Clint, Andy Goff, Eric Drobotij, Jim Gallagher, and Mike Schmidt (who were reunited from the successful Steel City teams) of winning two consecutive national championships was unique in the annals of Pennsylvania amateur baseball history. Mike's kids played as hard as he had lived. Lots of dirty uniforms after a game. But every player on those teams had already inherited a sense of respect for opponents, umpires, and the game itself. The experience was a perfect union of maturing personalities and baseball talent. A sports reporter asked Mike for the key to his success in bringing consecutive national championships to Western Pennsylvania. He responded, "Nobody treated anybody else like superstars; they all had to work for things. They respected each other. Everyone knew their roles."

Clint particularly appreciated and thrived his first year from his association with the team co-captains and natural leaders, Jason Zoeller, now an attorney, and Warren Schaeffer, now a coach in the Colorado Rockies' minor league system. The exposure to natural leaders at that age was valuable.

Among the life lessons that can be learned on the baseball diamond is the emergence of leadership and the ability to follow those whose leadership instills confidence. It was never in sharper focus than in the semifinals of the national NABF championship tournament in London, Ontario, in 2003. Midway through the game, Mike succumbed to an outburst at an umpire and found himself ejected from the game. So there was the team, facing a "win or go home" game in the middle innings with no coach. But none of them seemed concerned. There certainly was no panic. The player-leaders huddled in the dugout to make some adjustments to how signals would be relayed. An important pitching change a couple innings later was handled effectively by the players and secured the win. The ability of these young men to accept the challenge without an ounce of panic or concern was obvious to all observing the game. They didn't miss a beat, won the game, and won the following championship game against the Orlando Scorpions 9–7 (with their coach on the bench for the duration).

That following year in Jackson, Mississippi, at the NABF 18U nationals, Coach Kosko's team again demonstrated their poise and composure. The team (by then called the Bulldogs) came back from a five-run deficit to win its semi-final game, and won another come-from-behind effort in the championship game in extra innings against the Indiana Bulls. That would be the last baseball game that Clint and Andy would play as teammates.

Mike Kosko was their man. The team was his life. When each of those two seasons was over, there was no doubt how his players felt about Coach Kosko. At the end of the successful 18U season, he gave Clint (and I expect the others) a handwritten sheet with guidance for navigating through college and into adult life. When Clint arrived at his EKU dorm room, it was the first thing he unpacked and pinned to his corkboard.

Clint being waved home by Coach Mike Kosko

Clint, Coach Kosko, and NABF championship trophy
(18U), 2004, Jackson, Mississippi

SIX

Division I College Baseball: The EKU Years

"I aspire to be seen by people as I saw Clint."
—JAYSON LANGFELS, friend and EKU teammate,
currently third baseman for the Tulsa Drillers,
the Colorado Rockies' AA team

As a teenager, Clint's baseball goal was to earn a scholarship to play at the Division I level. Excellent opportunities exist at the Division II and III levels at countless colleges offering excellent baseball and academic programs. But Clint had an intense desire to play at what he regarded as the highest level of college competition. He accepted a four-year scholarship to Eastern Kentucky University in the Division I Ohio Valley Conference (OVC).

The transition from high school baseball to college baseball is challenging. Everyone was a high school star. Clint would be living six hours from home, attempting to balance the demands of college academics, plus all of the normal adjustments to college life, and the challenge of participating in a baseball program that included practices or games most of the academic year. Some believe that no college sport is more demanding of a student-athlete's time than

Freshman season at EKU

baseball. Teams play about sixty games per year (more than any other college sport), roughly half on the road, and the OVC stretched from Missouri to Illinois to Alabama, which meant lots of long bus rides (for which Clint was routinely the last player on the bus—but never late).

"I met Clint in 2005 when I was just a freshman on the EKU women's varsity soccer team and we were in study hall. Clint introduced me to some of the other baseball players, and I introduced him to the soccer girls. By the time college was over, we had become a group of friends with an unbreakable bond. Through hardships and good times, we were all always there for each other. I can remember countless conversations with Clint that went on for hours but felt like minutes because he was just so incredible to listen to and

*talk to that the time would go by so quickly, and by the end
my cheeks would be hurting from laughing so much."*

—LINDSAY ISMER, friend

College players who are not drafted into professional
baseball frequently take five or six years to earn a degree,
given the diminished number of credit hours in their spring
semesters. But Clint graduated in four years, and he was
justifiably proud of that accomplishment. Instead of playing
in the summer "wood bat" leagues, he would use the summer for an additional course or a required internship.

For all four years, Clint's head coach was Elvis Dominguez, a proud Cuban-American citizen born in Cienfuegos
in 1964. He eventually joined his parents on one of the last
"Freedom Flights" from Havana to Miami, the largest re-
settlement program of political refugees ever sponsored by
the United States government, offering an escape from
Fidel Castro's Cuba to 265,000 people. While the Catholic
Church attempted to relocate the refugees throughout the
country, most settled in Miami and made a profoundly positive impact upon that region.

Elvis grew up in Miami and became the first member of
his family to attend college by earning a baseball scholarship
to Creighton University, the Jesuit college in Omaha, Ne-
braska, from which he earned his degree and launched his
baseball-coaching career. He served as the EKU head coach
from 2001 to 2008. He was particularly proud that in each
of his last five years at EKU, his teams posted at least a 3.0
grade point average. Clint was a "Colonel Scholar" several
of those semesters.

Elvis's heritage shaped his effectiveness as a college coach.
He was grateful for the opportunities that had been afforded
him by his adopted country, and he continually stressed to
his players the appreciation they should feel for the good

With Coach Dominguez at Senior Recognition Day, 2008

fortune of being born into the greatest country on Earth, an appreciation that no American should take for granted.

One of the many adjustments to playing college baseball is that for most freshmen, they are playing for the first time for full-time professional coaches whose livelihood and that of their families depends on how successful they are at their job. Fortunately, many programs define coaching success by assessing a broader array of criteria than wins and losses on the diamond, meaning that those coaches constantly press their players for academic accomplishment, responsible behavior, and character development, in addition to performance on the field.

On Clint's official recruiting visit, he was hosted by the players, but Mary and I accompanied him since we had never been to the EKU campus. While Mary and I watched preparation for the day's game at Turkey Hughes Field, the university president, Joanne Glasser, walked by the field.

Coach Dominguez ambled over to make sure that Mary and I were introduced to the president, which led to a pleasant extended chat. She was a baseball fan, interested in the university's program, and a big fan of Coach Dominguez. She stressed how well she had come to know Elvis and to appreciate how well he fulfilled all of his coaching responsibilities, not just those measured by wins and losses. She concluded by telling Mary that she would love to have a son play for a team coached by Elvis Dominguez. She was right.* Clint also valued his relationship with John Corbin, the EKU pitching coach. Although not Clint's "position coach," he was consistently supportive of Clint all four years, and Clint enjoyed the time they were able to spend together.†

During the team orientation program in the fall of Clint's first semester, Coach Dominguez asked him, "Which of your new teammates is least like you?" Clint thought it was an odd question, but it wasn't difficult for Clint to respond with Joe Oliver's name. They had played against each other in the NABF championship tournament in Jackson, Mississippi, that summer, but Clint had found it difficult to connect personally with Joe in the fall as much as he would have liked. Joe and Clint had arrived at EKU (Joe from Chicago and Clint from Pittsburgh) via much different avenues. Joe had faced challenges growing up in inner-city Chicago that Clint had never endured in suburban Pittsburgh. Their immediate family support structures were much different. Joe seemed at first more serious and introverted, while Clint was more engaging.

Before the season began in the spring, Coach Dominguez announced the travel roommate pairings. Clint and Joe

---

* When President Glasser later became president of Bradley University, it did not take long for her to convince Coach Dominguez to join her team at Bradley in 2008.

† Coach Corbin joined Coach Dominguez at Bradley in 2008.

were paired together. Recalling his comment to the coach in the fall, Clint asked me how he could have been paired with someone so (superficially at least) unlike him. Before I had a chance to respond, Clint caught himself. In a flash of insight, he just nodded at me and said, "I think I get it." I took the opportunity to advise him that I have developed some of my most valued friendships with people who initially or superficially appeared not to be cut from the same cookie cutter as was I. He did not need to be told.

Clint and Joe remained road trip roommates for all four seasons. Their relationship developed steadily into a strong friendship. They learned from each other in a natural, evolutionary process. Eventually, as I observed Clint and Joe spending time together on the bench or after a game or enjoying dinner together with me on the road, the subtle

Joe Oliver and Clint, sporting senior players' bleached hair

wisdom of their head coach became more apparent. I believe Clint and Joe were the only members of the 2004 recruiting class to graduate in four years.

As with all of his prior teams, Clint made many friends among his EKU teammates, senior or junior to him. Since they were sharing the college experience and a more rigorous schedule of baseball activities away from their comfort zones, their shared experiences created strong bonds.

Clint became a close friend of Christian Friedrich, the talented left-handed pitcher who became the number one draft pick of the Colorado Rockies in 2008. They stayed in constant contact through social media and video games after

With Christian Friedrich

Christian's "Yinzer 24" glove he uses when he takes the mound for the Colorado Rockies (photo by Christian Friedrich)

EKU. They visited each other's cities (Chris was from Chicago) for hockey games in the winter, usually accompanied by Aaron Barrows, another EKU teammate from Chicago. Clint and Chris developed a unique and strong friendship sourced in the common experiences they shared playing for the Colonels. Christian will never forget Clint, their valued friendship, and Clint's constant support as Chris battled through a series of injuries that threatened to disrupt his major league pitching career.

> *"Clint is the brother Christian never had, and I'm grateful for the joy he brought my son, even though it was only a short time. Clint just had that ability to make you grin!"*
>
> —BILL FRIEDRICH, friend and father of Christian Friedrich

Chris revealed to me recently that during the Colorado Rockies' pregames, "there comes a moment that starts with sadness, then fear, and is followed by anger. Only for a half-second though. I am reminded of something we used to say to each other, and any number of instances happen that remind me of my best bud. But then I look to the sky and tell him I miss him and thank him for sharing his life with me."

That is my hero. That is my friend.

Another teammate, Frank Krailler, settled in Cincinnati after graduation, and Nick Barte stayed in Richmond to teach high school math and coach baseball, so it was not difficult for them to gather in Cincinnati (for a Steelers game or when Christian and the Rockies were in town to play the Reds). And they and Christian and Justin Fitz enjoyed fishing experiences wherever they could be found.

Many EKU teammates reluctantly made their way to Charleston or Pittsburgh to say goodbye to a friend they expected to enjoy for decades.

"Clint was not only a great teammate but a great friend. Anytime Clint was around, he lit up the room. We shared so many great memories on and off the field at EKU. I will cherish the times we spent on the diamond, at the local creek fishing, and hanging out."

—Brett Bolger, friend and EKU teammate

"He was truly one in a million."

—Shane Zegarac, friend and EKU teammate

Clint's baseball years at EKU were successful. He hit a solid .270 for his career there. He had a five RBI game against Tennessee Tech and a five-hit game against Eastern Illinois. He always remembered a pinch-hit double against Tennessee at Lindsey Nelson Stadium his freshman year. And with two teammates, he accomplished something I had never seen—a "back-to-back-to-back": three home runs on three consecutive pitches, with Dylan McMaine batting before him and Shawn Flora following him.

The team was always competitive, although it never won an OVC championship during Clint's four years. He particularly enjoyed the spring trips to Bradenton, Florida, where

Back-to-back-to-back: Shawn Flora, Clint, and Dylan McMaine after their three home runs on three consecutive pitches

the team was able to compete against teams from nearly every conference, including the SEC, Big Ten, Ivy League, Patriot Conference, Atlantic 10, Big East, Big Sun, Southern Conference, Conference USA, and others. And it coincided with spring training there for Neil Walker and the Pirates, giving the pair of buddies a welcome opportunity to enjoy a dinner or a trip to the mall to leave baseball behind for a couple hours and enjoy some quality time together.

He also enjoyed the midweek games against nonconference opponents, including Tennessee, Marshall, Dayton, Cincinnati, Miami, and others. Clint had acquaintances or former teammates on many of those teams, so he particularly enjoyed that competition. Former teammates Chris Koutsavlis (Mt. Lebanon) and Adam Dobies (Mid-Atlantic Rookies) pitched for Marshall, so Clint always hoped he would have a chance to bat against them.

"I am happy to have shared so many great memories with Clint in high school as well as in college. I always made sure to travel to midweek games when we played EKU so I could

get a chance to see him and catch up. I know when I walk through those pearly gates Clint will greet me with a joke or two to remind me why I liked him so much!"

—Chris Koutsavlis, friend, Mt. Lebanon teammate, and competitor at Marshall University

The last day of Clint's senior season at EKU was a doubleheader at home on Senior Recognition Day. It started with a pregame public embrace at home plate from Coach Elvis Dominguez and ended with a good, long cry as Clint hugged his mother way down the foul line in the bullpen out of public view. He had known since he woke that morning that these would be his last baseball games. As if on cue, he went five for five in the first game (an accomplishment I had never witnessed, even in youth baseball). And then—again as if on cue—he went hitless in the second game of his last baseball day.

Surely, the Baseball Gods were sending a message: Baseball will offer unparalleled joy conjoined with occasional defeats. Yet, in that bullpen, the bittersweet tears of regret that he and his mother shed—now that this important phase of his life was complete—were overwhelmed by tears of joy for a game that he so loved.

The next six years of his life were even more reaffirming for his parents. His athletic outlets evolved toward running, golf, and fitness training. But the baseball lessons continued to influence a maturing process over those six years that validated all of the effort that he and his family had invested in the game he so enjoyed. Everyone noticed how mature, self-confident, and engaging he had become, particularly among adults—even those he had just met.

He had nothing but success in his initial employment opportunities, and he was genuinely enthusiastic about his most recent opportunity with the Charleston office of

Merrill Lynch. He regarded this one as right in his sweet spot, one he could hit for extra bases. After completing the required exams and licensing, he felt that the person he had become—the unique character and personality molded by the baseball and initial employment experiences and successes—was well suited for this next challenge.

"Strength and Confidence"

"Carly's Christmas sox making me the best dressed in the office today" (Clint on Facebook)

Lucky, Mary, Clint at EKU

All eyes on the ball

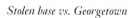

Stolen base vs. Georgetown

Locked and loaded

Comparing notes with Tennessee Tech's Thomas Nelson

At Morehead State

Lift off!

It has a chance

Extra bases against Henry Mabee of Morehead State

Avoiding the tag

Clint Unvarnished

Born To Run

"The only way to truly conquer something, is to love it" -40%

"The heroes of the past are untouchable, protected forever by the fortress door of time."

"If I have a swing, I have a chance" Bobbe Watson

"They were expected to accomplish nothing so they could try anything"

Kerouac - Dharma Bums
Charles Bukowski

"Capable of absolutely anything except Moderation"

Carly, Clint, Mary, Don
at Seabrook

Carly, Don, Clint at Seabrook

Carly and Clint

Clint and Don

Clint and Carly at Burgettstown

Carly, Mary, Clint at Seabrook

Clint and Carly

Clint's 28th birthday, with Juliana, Alex, Caroline, Mary, Carly, and Fin

Clint and Carly, Soglio, Switzerland 1996

Carly, Mary, Clint, London 1997

Clint, Mary, Carly, Switzerland 1998

Mary, Clint, Carly, Pompeii 1998

Clint and Carly with Najette

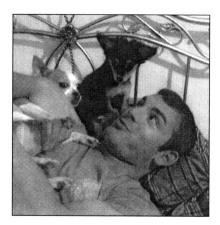

Clint with Lucky and Elvis at EKU

Clint with Fin at Newburn

Fin taking his first ride

Clint with Barry Bonds

Clint with Ryan Eckenrode

Clint with Steve Basheda

"Once Upon a Lifetime"

Once upon a lifetime.
Two souls intertwined,
A tapestry of love,
Woven over time.
Two souls searching,
They know not when or why
They will find each other again.

Though sometimes lost along the way,
Their thoughts for each other
Are never far away.
Two missing pieces to a puzzle.
No words, just a glance of our eyes.
Somewhere in time.
We'll be together again,
You and I.
Once upon a lifetime.

—Clint Seymour

*Becky with Clint and
his parents at Amel's*

Clint and Becky "selfie"

*Clint and Becky at
Bohicket Marina,
Seabrook*

*Becky, Clint at Marye Beasley
and Richard Kohn's wedding*

Becky, Don, and Clint in Pittsburgh

*Clint and Becky with Niki and
Neil Walker, Hannah, Ty*

Clint and Becky

*Mary, Becky, Clint, and Don
on Bay Street*

"Midsummer Eve"

At last, when all the summer's shine is met with the cool night
    breeze,
The sun has come to meet the forging depths of the horizon.
At last, with the stars aligned in the sky,
The day has concluded, and night is upon me.
A cool breeze rushes quickly through the trees, and sets my
    heart ablaze.
At last, right has been done.

—Clint Seymour

*Clint with a red drum
on the Bohicket*

Clint with Raelyn

Clint and Alex "selfie"

Clint with Misty

Clint and Misty "selfie"

Clint and Misty at EKU party

Mardi

"Undiscovered"

My hopes are so high that your kiss might kill me,
So won't you kill me so I'd die happy.
My heart is yours to fill or burst
To break or bury
Or wear as jewelry
Whichever you prefer.
The words are hushed lest not get busted
Just lay entwined here undiscovered.

—*Clint Seymour*

"The First Time"

I never was struck before that hour,
With love so sudden and so sweet.
Her face bloomed as a flower,
And stole my heart away complete.

My face turned pale, a deadly pale.
My legs began to sway.
And when her essence came unveiled,
My essence turned to clay.

And then my blood rushed to my face,
And took my eyesight far away.
The trees and bushes round the place
Seemed midnight at noonday.

I could not see a single thing.
Words from my eyes did start.
They spoke as chords do from the string
And blood burnt round my heart.

Are flowers the winter's choice?
Is love's bed always snow?
She seemed to hear my silent voice,
To sense a heart aglow.

I never saw so sweet a face
As that I stood before.
My heart has left its dwelling place
And can return no more.

—Clint Seymour

First uniform

Clint with the "Hardware"

With Mary and Carly at West Mifflin

Mt. Lebanon Travel Team (back) Goff, Bannon, Dattilo, Snead, Leckenby, Barber, Franchick, (front) Millhouse, Brown, Shingle, Kerr, Zych, Seymour, Tickle

Clint Seymour

Andy Goff

Dale Mollenhauer

Neil Walker

Eric Drobotij

Jim Gallagher

Ty Haak

Bob Kohl

NABF National Champions (18U) 2003, Ontario

NABF National Champions (18U) 2004, Mississippi

Mary and Clint at his high school graduation, June 2004

*Clint with coach and teacher
Patt McCloskey*

*Eric Drobotij, Coach Mark
Saghy, Andy Goff, Clint*

I'll never know what would have happened had Emily not discovered Sarah and me scurrying from the party for the door that October night. As the leaves fell outside, we remained inside. The night would end as it had started. Same old guy with the same old feelings about the same old girl. Sarah and I talked the rest of the night, always under the watchful eye of Emily.

"I'll be right back," I said to her as I pushed my chair back from the kitchen table. My leg was falling asleep and I needed to stretch. I smiled to myself as I walked over to the window. I looked up and saw the moon, and it was as bright as ever. I'm sure the air was just cool enough that if you breathed hard you could see your breath vanishing into the clear night air. I imagined being out on the street somewhere with Sarah. For once, my dream wasn't so far from a reality. It was three feet away. We would have joked around most of the way back to her house, because that's just how our relationship was. Staring up at the full moon, we'd chase our shadows all the way back to her basement. But not tonight. What a night it would have been, I thought, as I turned back to the kitchen table. There was Sarah, sitting there. She didn't notice me. I turned back to the window, shaking my head. I looked back up at the moon again and wondered if there would be another time. I told myself there would be another time. I turned back again to the table, but this time Sarah was gone.

POSTSCRIPT: Clint would be pleased to know that Sarah, now married, traveled a long distance to attend his memorial service in Pittsburgh on May 12, 2014, a few days after his twenty-eighth birthday.

Contact!

Heading to first

Clint with Coach Elvis Dominguez

Clint with Matt Davis

Brush-back

With young fans at Turkey Hughes Field

High fives

Ready to launch

Tools of the trade

Home run tribute

Pausing at second

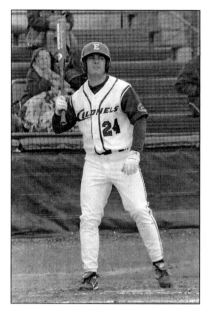

"Wish I had that pitch back"

It has a chance

"Atta boy"

Waiting for the sign

Clint's presence with Uncle Rich at 15,000 feet in the Andes, en route to Machu Picchu

Clint's uncle Rich Seymour and cousin Owen Vogel (wearing Clint's hat and shirt) at Machu Picchu (photos by Richard A. Seymour)

SEVEN

The Two-Strike Hit

"Whether you think you can or whether you think you can't, you're right."

—Clint's Facebook post on November 10, 2011

Baseball devotees recognize that in the tantalizingly intense personal battle between batter and pitcher, the batter is disadvantaged once he has two strikes on him. Subsequent counts are "pitcher's counts." It is axiomatic in professional baseball that no one makes his living repeatedly trying to hit with two strikes in the count. Throughout his career, Clint thrived on the two-strike pitch. Once he had reached the baseball level where this would normally be a differentiator, I would repeatedly suggest to Clint that he needed to avoid getting behind in the count. I never convinced him, despite showing him Ted Williams's book (*The Science of Hitting*) and a baseball metrics article tracking major league hitters' success against various counts. His view was that he would put the same good swing on a pitch in the strike zone regardless of the count . . . and, by the way, he benefitted from seeing more pitches in deeper counts. So one season I actually tracked Clint's statistics, ultimately realizing that he fared as well with two strikes in the count as

The two-strike swing

he did when he was ahead in the count. I had been proven wrong, and Clint's simpler approach of attacking each pitch the same way continued to be his trademark. I then busied myself with understanding how this mindset had developed.

From his earliest baseball days, Clint was strongly motivated to learn the game and its skills, but his parents and his early coaches also emphasized the joy of playing and interacting with new friends. That joy kept him interested, which in turn kept him attending practices, which in turn resulted in success, which produced more enjoyment. Not an uncommon cycle. Beginning at such an early age kept him insulated from the introduction of "pressure" into the game. The foundations laid by his early baseball experiences never really changed much. It was always fun. It always introduced new friends. There was enough challenge to motivate him to continue to improve. And he always knew that a "failure" would be followed by a new opportunity.

He eventually became quite competitive, and his desire to succeed thrived. But it remained fun. During a game in the

Ohio Valley Conference championship tournament in 2007, his good friend Christian Friedrich was pitching and Clint was playing first base. On a routine grounder back to the mound, Chris delivered a strike to Clint at first, only to have the webbing in Clint's mitt tear, allowing the runner to reach first safely. Having never seen this happen before, Chris and Clint looked at each other, shrugged, and smiled, suppressing a giggle. No one on the team was more competitive than Chris or Clint, but they understood that the only response was to retire the next batter. And they did.

His success at hitting with two strikes eventually injected itself into Clint's post-baseball DNA. Baseball at an early age without pressure instilled in him an inner peace that allowed him to face a two-strike pitch with courage and confidence, not fear. He believed that, as golfer Bubba Watson says, "If I have a swing, I have a chance." After all, his swing was as good as the pitcher's pitch, regardless of the count. It became intuitive to approach sales calls and business challenges the same way. What a gift from parents and coaches who let him develop a personality that was immune to pressure, confident in his abilities, and with the courage to await the opportunity of the next at bat.

"Clint loved you and was extremely fortunate to be blessed with you, the perfect parents for Clint. No one could have done a better job. You allowed Clint to be himself, where others may have forced him into a preconceived model of what he should be. You saw Clint as the free spirit that he was, and allowed him to mature and grow on his timeline, not the measuring stick of others; and you were rewarded for it by the kind, caring young man he became."

—Jim Haak, friend and coach,
in his May 7, 2014, eulogy in Charleston

In the same way that Clint could not understand why hitting with two strikes was an issue, he also could not understand why business colleagues and others let pressures and challenges cause their behavior to impede their effectiveness. He assured prospective employers that his record brimmed with success; that there was no quit in him; and that any challenge would be met by him as an 0–2 count that he could transform into a base hit, as he had since he was six years old.

"If there is one thing that stood out about Clint's game to me . . . it was that he could hit with two strikes (and Don, I had written this independently before you spoke it at the Charleston service). With two strikes, you have to be prepared for anything, and you are one mistake away from sitting down. Clint could foul off a fastball on the corner, spit on a curveball in the dirt, watch a change-up, foul off a curveball, watch a fastball in, and then once he finally got a pitch he liked, drive a triple to right center field. It's almost like he preferred this.

And it translated into his personal adult life. Some people may assume that what I'm saying is that Clint could perform with his back against the wall. That's not what I'm saying, as there isn't much evidence to support that. He didn't spend much time there. What I'm suggesting is that to hit with two strikes as often and as well as he did, you need to be carefree, and you need to have an amazing sense of self-confidence. You need to suspend all care of consequence, and if there was one thing Clint never really cared for, it was negative consequences."

—TYLER HAAK, friend and teammate, in his May 12, 2014, eulogy at Clint's Pittsburgh memorial service

EIGHT

Acrophobia

"In a world of people trying to fit in and conform, Clint would have none of it. Clint didn't march to the beat of a different drummer—Clint wouldn't march for anybody. He danced and glided through life. I much admired Clint's approach to life. He left stress, structure, and the hamster wheel to us less fortunate and celebrated life on his terms."

—JIM HAAK, friend and coach,
in his May 7, 2014, eulogy in Charleston

I t was the summer of 1998, and the Steel City Wildcats were headed to Mississauga, Ontario, for a weekend tournament, when we stopped at Niagara Falls to provide a brief side-trip for the boys. One of our sightseeing stops was a gondola ride several hundred feet above the Great Gorge of the violent Niagara River. Jim Ellis Sr. jumped on board to chaperone (the players expected that of Jim). I stayed back on dry land (the players expected that of me). Clint had inherited from me a serious fear of heights. All of the other players rushed into the waiting gondola with enthusiasm, trying to swing it back and forth, announcing that it would be "just like Kennywood" (a Western Pennsylvania amusement park), no doubt at Ellis Sr.'s urging. But Clint was inching his way down the ramp toward the gondola, hesitating with each tiny step. I was, of course, well aware of Clint's inherited fear of heights. A parent's dilemma . . . my son is frozen in fear, but no twelve-year-old wants his father interceding in front of his teammates to protect him from the terror that they relished. As I paused, frozen in terror of a different nature, Neil Walker departed the gondola, and walked back up the ramp to Clint. "I don't do very well with heights, Clint, will you stay here with me?" I finally exhaled and brushed away a tear from my eye. My guess is that neither Clint nor Neil remembered the moment by that evening—it was so natural—but it stuck with me. I had no experience with twelve-year-olds prior to that season, but I was learning fast from them. Assemble the right group, give them an opportunity on the diamond to build relationships that transform teammates into respected friends, and then stay out of the way and watch the magic.

Clint and Neil in Canada, circa 1998

Fast-forward to 2003. Mike Kosko's BP team was playing in the national NABF 18U championship in London, Ontario. On an off-day, a group of parents led the team to an abandoned stone quarry outside of town, with crystal clear water and razor-sharp walls at its edges. The boys quickly changed into bathing suits and dashed toward a path that would lead them to an apex from which a swan dive into the clear, azure waters awaited them. Clint confided to Jason Zoeller, one of the senior team leaders, that it was admittedly a beautiful setting, but that he was afraid of heights, couldn't dive, and couldn't swim so well either. I was some distance away, but in desperation I asked myself, "Where's Neil?"* Jason said confidently and reassuringly, "Just follow me, and we'll have Warren [Schaeffer] wait for you in the water." Clint—now seventeen—scaled the path behind Jason, and on his turn positioned himself for what would become his customary entry into any swimming venue: the legs-first jump while tightly clenching the nostrils with the thumb and index finger of the right hand. Once he surfaced and paddled with Warren back to shore, he let out an exuberant scream of accomplishment and followed Jason back up the path.

On August 10, 2014, Clint's friend and cousin Brian Seymour—who had never before climbed a mountain—revealed to me that "Clint set his fear of heights aside last week to help me through one of the most grueling, terrifying, awesome, and beautiful experiences of my life. He stood with me on August 7 on top of Mount Rainier in Washington." Brian had carried Clint's memorial service photo with him and placed it in the capsule at the summit, signing in as "Brian and Clint Seymour 8-7-2014."

---

* Neil was playing for Team USA in the Junior Pan-Am Cup in the late summer of 2003.

Brian Seymour on Mt. Rainier, August 7, 2014 (photos by Brian Seymour)

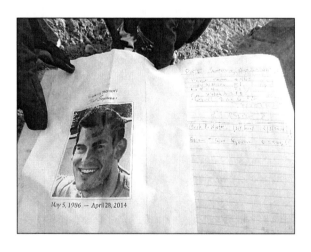

NINE

SoHo

---

*"Clint: Today [at your May 12 memorial service in Pittsburgh],
I witnessed something amazing . . .
In a moment of darkness, I saw light.
In the confusion of loss, I saw the clarity of love.
And in the face of a tragedy, I saw hope.
Seeing all of the wonderful people gathered in your name today,
whose lives you touched and inspired, made me remember some-
thing most of us, too often, forget—
in the end, only kindness matters.
Thank you for being a genuine example of this, and all that is
good in the world.
You and your family are loved. God bless."*

—Chelsia Krejocic, posted on Clint's
Facebook page on May 12, 2014

If the Sam Malone character from the sitcom *Cheers* relocated to Pittsburgh, he would have tended bar at SoHo. And what a pair he and Clint would have made.

After his college graduation in 2008, Clint was not yet interested in a "real job," and he thought that a bartending job at the right kind of establishment would develop his people skills—particularly with adults, who at times intimidated him a bit. So he went to bartending school and was hired by Karen Weil, the manager of SoHo, the upscale bar and grill across the street from PNC Park, home of the Pittsburgh Pirates, and down the street from Heinz Field, home of the Pittsburgh Steelers.

The proximity to PNC Park naturally allowed Clint to make friends with some of the Pirates front office folks who would have lunch there or stop for a drink and a snack after work. Recently acquired Pirates players often stayed at the adjoining hotel, ate their meals at SoHo, and enjoyed Clint's company and his baseball background. And his friend Neil Walker was called up to the Pirates shortly after Clint started working there. Clint enjoyed working occasionally with Pirates marketing and public relations personnel, selling team memorabilia and artifacts for Pirates charities at events. Most of his numerous friends in the 'Burgh attended Pirates or Steelers games regularly, so rarely did an evening go by without a friend (old or new) stopping by. It was a match made in heaven. Clint flourished quite naturally in his goal of developing confidence levels and friendships with new adult friends, as well as the many contemporaries whose friendship he valued. The ease with which he quickly developed relationships would serve him well when he launched into his next career in business-to-business sales.

> *"Clint was like a magnet, attracting everyone to him."*
>
> —TIP POHL, friend

> *"They might as well have renamed SoHo as 'Clint's Place.' We stopped there all the time before Pirates games because Clint was there with a hug and a smile. I will never pass there again without thinking of him."*
>
> —CAROLYN WALKER, friend

Clint was joined at the hip with Nate M'Sadoques, another SoHo bartender, who became a close friend of Clint's and many of Clint's friends. Clint and Nate made quite a pair behind the bar. Nate helped Clint infuse his gift of joy and enthusiasm into *all* of the relationships he naturally developed with management, coworkers, customers of all ages, and eventually to clients and potential clients in his next sales job.

"When Clint decided to join his family by moving to Charleston, I was truly sad. He left me a letter that I will cherish always, about how much influence I had on his life and how he would be forever grateful. Well, if the truth be told, I just allowed him to grow and flourish, and it was Clint who impacted my life by showing me how to enjoy it. . . . Clint, we will be naming a drink on our new cocktail menu for you. Every time we make it or drink it, we will remember our friend, our partner, our angel. Love you."

—KAREN WEIL, SoHo manager, posted on
Clint's Facebook page on April 29, 2014

SoHo did create a drink (actually, it may have been a recipe concocted by Clint) called the "Seymour" in his honor, with a portion of each sale being donated to Pirates charities and the Clint Seymour "Play Ball" Fund. The drink was rolled out on Cinco de Mayo, which would have been Clint's twenty-eighth birthday. From our back porch in South Carolina, I instantly sent Karen a photo of our family launching twenty-eight balloons over the salt marsh Clint loved, in honor of his birthday. Karen was able to display the picture on the screen, to the delight of the roomful of Clint's friends who had gathered for the occasion. Neil quietly donated an autographed shirt and bat that were raffled off, raising ad-

"The Seymour" leading the drink menu
at SoHo

ditional thousands of dollars for the charities and Clint's "Play Ball" Fund. Clint's good friend and teammate Keenan Klett purchased the first twenty-four Seymour drinks served at SoHo that day in honor of Clint's favorite jersey number. The last I heard, sales were brisk, particularly among the ladies.

I cannot walk through SoHo without being approached (usually multiple times) by friends of Clint previously unknown to me, each recounting uncommon stories woven from common threads.

After the enormous celebration of love for Clint at his Pittsburgh memorial service at PNC Park's Hall of Fame, which was attended by 325 friends and family, Karen Weil sent another farewell to an employee who had become so much more than that:

"We have many branches on our tree of life. Yesterday this branch got stronger as we said goodbye to a member of it. What we walked away with was a renewal of living every day to the fullest, remembering to give away smiles like it was our business, and not forgetting to tell those on your tree that you love them. Clint Seymour, your legacy will live on in each of us—that I can promise. To all the branches of my tree—my kids, my siblings, my friends, SoHo, etc. Thank you for always living this life with me and may we all remember to stay in the batter's box, even with two strikes, and then hit a triple like Clint. Love to all."

—Karen Weil, SoHo manager, posted on
Clint's Facebook page on May 13, 2014

Nate and Clint at Soho

Clint and Jess Davis at SoHo

TEN

Born to Run

Laura was feeling exasperated in the parking lot outside Merrill Lynch's Lockwood Drive office. She had raised the hood of her car, but couldn't twist off the cap that she needed to remove. Clint was walking by and saw her struggling. He quietly approached the car, twisted the cap off, and before she could thank him, he simply shrugged and proclaimed in his trademark deadpan with lips curling toward a smile, "I am the strongest man in the world" as he continued toward his car.

Upon graduation from EKU, Clint filled the space baseball had taken in his life with ease. He became more devoted to physical fitness and a regular gym regimen; he returned to his hockey passion (teaming up with Andy to play in adult leagues); he pursued golf with fresh intensity; he found a mixed doubles tennis partner in his mother, Mary; and he fished relentlessly. But, principally, he developed a passion for running. It was a perfect fit. Outside his comfort zone, it offered him an athletic challenge. Since he never pursued anything without setting lofty goals, he eventually was able to push himself to run the Pittsburgh marathon. "Twenty-six miles on my twenty-sixth birthday" became his 2012 mantra. Predictably, he succeeded, running a respectable 3:40. I was in Pittsburgh that day, although I had declined his challenge to run sixty-six miles on my sixty-sixth birthday. I followed him as well as I could by driving to designated checkpoints to proudly watch him fulfill his goal.

"I'll never forget in 2012 when Clint and I trained for the half marathon in Pittsburgh. For a month or two, I'd drive down to Mt. Lebanon or he'd drive into the city, and we'd run, put our headphones in, and talk about whatever. About three weeks before the race, Clint told me that he was going to run the full. Some would call this putting yourself into a two-strike count, considering most marathoners restructure their diets, use books to train for six months, and aren't a 180-pound mass of muscle running down the street. Clint ran the full marathon in under 3:40. As I lay in bed midday resting off my 2:10 half, he sent me a picture message of a twenty-four pack of Tecate for Cinco de Mayo."

—TYLER HAAK, friend and teammate,
in his May 12, 2014, eulogy in Pittsburgh

Clint continued to run regularly in Pittsburgh and in Charleston after his move there in 2013. He planned to run other marathons until he qualified for Boston. Both Pittsburgh and Charleston offered scenic venues to fuel Clint's running passion, with rivers and bridges galore. As he studied for his securities licensing exams upon joining Merrill Lynch, the only diversion from his intense study regimen was for regular mind-clearing runs. He particularly enjoyed taking a change of clothes to work and running a round-trip across the majestic Ravenel Bridge after work.

As with most runners, he found his running hours to be tranquil and mentally refreshing, even Zen-like. He told me that the biggest challenge was getting his mind in shape as well as his body. And, of course, as with all runners, the rewards were a similar confluence of the mental and the physical. Running also offered opportunities to join with friends (male or female) for those special peaceful hours.

His passion for fishing offered much the same release as running, and he pursued it tirelessly. As with running, he could enjoy it alone for hours, privately letting his mind wander; or he could enjoy the company of his many friends with a line in the water.

Another athletic passion he pursued after EKU was golf. While he played when he could in Pittsburgh with friends, including Andy and Neil when possible, his golfing fervor reached its peak when he was in South Carolina, whether visiting us after our 2011 move or upon his relocation to Charleston in the fall of 2013. His uncle Chuck Rudek inherited his clubs, and he reports that his game has never been more successful or more meaningful.

Start of the 2012 Pittsburgh Marathon

*Pittsburgh Marathon
2012 attire (Becky's
registered shirt)*

*Pittsburgh Marathon—
Carson Street*

*Pittsburgh Marathon—Fifth
Avenue*

*A pause on Pittsburgh's West End
Bridge*

Ravenel Bridge, Charleston

With Christian Friedrich and a red drum

With Brian Seymour on the Bohicket

On the tee

"Playing through" on Kiawah's Ocean Course

ELEVEN

Lighting Up the World: The Source of Joy

As we were walking out of Andrew's restaurant in the Rivers Casino in Pittsburgh, I couldn't resist sliding into an empty chair at a blackjack table. At dinner I had told Clint that in my sporadic experience with the game, one of my few cardinal rules was always to split eights and aces. As he watched intently over my shoulder, on the first hand I was dealt a pair of eights. I split them, and won both hands. Next deal I received a pair of aces. Clint's eyes lit up. I split them, and won both hands again. I had made over a hundred dollars in less than a minute. Clint was in awe. But I quickly collected my chips, pushed away from the table, and cashed in, expecting Clint to absorb my lesson of quitting while ahead. As we waited for our car, I asked Clint, "So what did you learn tonight?" That mischievous smile emerged. "Let me guess. If you are enjoying something, it's time to stop."

Upon Clint's passing, his dear friend Niki Walker eloquently observed, "Clint lit up the world." That powerful sentiment has become embedded in me and has informed my recollection of the strengths of Clint's life, so essential to surviving his loss. And it was a sentiment that resonated through nearly all of the messages of condolence that we received from Clint's friends. Not dozens, not scores, but hundreds of messages, all lamenting the loss of someone who brought joy to their lives whenever they were in his company. And with the advent of social media, they could be in his company regularly. That capacity to bring joy to the lives of others was something I admired. It was something I envied. As Karen Weil said in a Facebook post:

"No matter how bad my day was, when Clint walked in, his smile would make it better. That charm I detected [when I hired him at SoHo] made him a favorite with the customers. He could tell a simple story that made you laugh. Some were outrageous; others were heartfelt. All were enjoyable. Everyone who met him fell in love. His presence made everyone age ninteteen to fifty-nine feel special, especially the ladies."

Or, as his friend and former coach Jim Haak put it:

"Of all the phone calls, emails, and texts that we receive in today's world, when I saw Clint Seymour's name pop up, I immediately smiled and chuckled. Before even opening it, I knew my day was about to get a little better, as Clint was sure to have a different perspective than the next guy."

And from a high school teacher:

"Clint was my very special student! He always made me laugh. What a love of life he had, and what a gift he possessed to make those around him laugh."

—JUDY OLSZEWSKI HULICK,
Mt. Lebanon High School teacher

That is my hero. That is my son.

It is natural to translate character-building on the baseball diamond into broader life lessons. Self-discipline and self-esteem are obvious examples. But—as the Clint Seymour "Play Ball" Fund will celebrate—one of the benefits of youth baseball (or soccer or hockey or marching band or Eagle Scouts) is even simpler: providing an opportunity to find *joy* in a communal setting. What was it about Clint's personality, his value set, his life experiences that permitted him effortlessly to infuse joy into the lives of others, including some who he did not know well? Ty Haak asked at his heartfelt May 12, 2014, eulogy of Clint, the same question:

> *"Of all the fantastic adults who were role models for Clint and me (and others) growing up—so many of whom are assembled here today at his memorial service—why do all of them admit to a desire to live more like the gallivanting, galvanizing joy boy I called my best friend? Why?"*

The answer to Ty's question may be found in the most common theme that emerges from the hundreds of messages from his friends—*the joy of being respected*, the joy of knowing that, whether they were in contact daily or infrequently and whether they were old friends or new friends, they remained important to Clint. Friends recalled that when he spoke to you, it was as if you were the only other person in the world.

> *"Clint was different. I will never meet anyone quite like him. When Clint talked to you, he made you feel important and that he genuinely cared about what you had to say."*
>
> —JAYSON LANGFELS, friend and EKU teammate
> (now playing AA ball for the Colorado Rockies)

> *"He understood me more than most. He always had a plan of attack for whatever life threw my way. He usually told me first off that it's going to be ok. He would always remind me*

that my attitude would usually determine my result. Always hinting to enjoy more. I miss him every day."

—CHRISTIAN FRIEDRICH, friend and EKU teammate
(now pitching for the Colorado Rockies)

Christian Friedrich pitching at EKU

Clint brought joy to people by *respecting* them.

When my father, Robert E. Seymour, came to Pittsburgh from Meadville, Pennsylvania, equipped only with a high school diploma, he found employment in 1939 as an entry-level clerk in the accounting department of a local natural gas utility. From his first day, he greeted the elevator operator, Dom, each morning with friendly banter. Three decades later, Dom would walk into my office at K&L Gates (well, actually, the law firm had a much longer name then; and my office was more of a cubicle), asking if I would assist him in connection with some legal work required as a result of the recent passing of his wife. We had never before met, and he was anxious to begin our attorney-client relationship with some background. He recounted meeting my father when both were beginning employment with the gas company. Dom's face lit up as he described to me how my father always remembered him and greeted him the same way over the years, as my father progressed through the company, eventually parlaying that high school diploma into the office of president of the company in 1963. He became emotional as he recounted to me how it felt to have a friend who treated him the same whether that friend was a bumbling novice or had reached the top of the corporate pinnacle. As I listened to Dom, I got the sense that he recognized that I found nothing that remarkable in his story. As well as I knew my father, it just never occurred to me that he would have interacted with Dom any other way over the years. Without needing to express the thought, Dom went on to volunteer to me how rare my father's quality was. After all, the elevator operator was the common denominator at the company—the only one interacting with every employee every day. And for Dom, his banter with the president during the morning elevator ride "lit up his life."

Robert E. Seymour

When Clint was old enough to absorb the story, I repeated it to him. He also found the story unremarkable, because it was so counterintuitive to him that any human would treat another deserving human without respect. The genes hadn't skipped a generation.

We received cards of condolence from two women who were mothers of daughters in Mt. Lebanon, each with a similar message. Each of their daughters had experienced some difficult times in school, with cruel taunts from some of the boys. Clint was an exception. He was always kind and friendly. And his being a boy with higher visibility in the class created even more joy from their interactions. Clint's grandfather and his friend Dom must be smiling.

Those two sensitive women each introduced their message to me with the preface that—unlike so many others—theirs had nothing to do with baseball. If they only knew.

From the time that Clint first ran onto a baseball diamond, it was natural for him to treat his teammates with respect. He had discovered the source of bringing joy into the lives of others for a few precious moments each day.

The elevator operator and the president.

Clint and Mary at Dixon and Molly Seymour's wedding

Crabfest fresh from the backyard creek

Bradenton spring trip, 2005

Clint and Elvis at Rockwood

TWELVE

The Joy of a Sister

"One of my first memories of Clint was when he went through Foodland on skates with a video camera on his head. I knew that he thought in a very special way even then."

—CLETE SMITH, friend

When Clint was almost three years old, he became a brother. Carly entered our world on a rainy Tuesday morning, without the drama that had preceded Clint's entrance. They brought joy into each other's lives, accompanied by the normal share of sibling friction. As they eased out of their tunnels of adolescence and started maturing into young adults, their relationship strengthened. They always had been each other's outlets for subjects that could not be discussed with parents. And as they matured—living some distance from each other but connected by the miracles of the digital age—they kept a loving, but not intruding, eye on each other's lives. They were starting to recognize and admire the respective strengths of their distinct personalities. Each was blessed with a keen sense of humor; Carly is less extroverted and more independent, strong, and resilient. Both made friends naturally—male and female—and treasured them.

135

More than anyone in our family, Carly loves celebrating her birthday (perhaps because she is the youngest). While she has always lived a modest life in San Antonio, Texas, she has been quick to remind us all of how many shopping days remained before the year's big event. And this year (2014), she reminded each of us that twenty-five was "a big one." Clint's assault occurred on the night of her twenty-fifth birthday. She traveled from San Antonio to Charleston (with her friend Lindsay Nagelhout for support) on the first flight available. And each day in Charleston, she found a private moment to call her place of employment to see if a package had arrived yet from her brother. Mary had told her that Clint had called the day before her birthday to get her business address so he could mail the birthday gift that he would be getting for her. But day after day, call after call, nothing had arrived.

About three weeks after the call, I needed to find a document from the glove compartment of Clint's car. When I opened it, I immediately saw a small yellow pouch, similar to those that the artisan jewelers in the Charleston market use to package a purchased item. I dashed upstairs and told Mary that I may have found the answer to Carly's birthday gift mystery. She opened it carefully and found a silver necklace with a pendant depicting the Angel Oak, a beautiful and ancient live oak tree located about midway between our home and Clint's on John's Island, and a favorite destination for visitors and those seeking spiritual renewal. We surmise that he bought it Friday (her birthday), or perhaps Thursday, and placed it in the glove compartment for safekeeping since he would be driving Friday evening as the designated driver when he and two friends went to King Street to enjoy the evening. Carly was ecstatic to finally receive her last birthday gift from her big brother. I reminded her that Clint would have reassured himself that as long as he had purchased the gift by her birthday, he was not tardy, regardless of when it was actually delivered.

Clint had been planning to visit Carly in San Antonio after he had settled into his new job with Merrill Lynch— just the two of them spending some bonding time together for a long weekend, maybe seeing some concerts, as they continued to ease into their relationship as adult siblings. That would have been nice. On April 25, 2014, before heading to work, Clint wished Carly an "awesome birthday" in a text message. It would be his last.

Carly and higher education had not been a match made in heaven. She could never understand why someone who wanted to be educated in fashion design (a strong program at Kent State) must study medieval history. It was a legitimate question to which I did not have a convincing answer. Her departure from the higher education environment led to an opportunity that she discovered with City Year, a federal program under the umbrella of VISTA (Volunteers in Service to America, aka the "domestic Peace Corps"). I had never heard of the program, but I was impressed that she had discovered the opportunity on her own and even more impressed with her motivation, as she explained it to Mary. "I didn't have much success in high school and even less in college. I want to spend some time now succeeding at something and accomplishing some good."

Quite independent of any external help from home or elsewhere, Carly did succeed and thrive in the San Antonio program, much of which involved helping Spanish-speaking preschoolers learn English. City Year asked her to return for a second year in more of a leadership role, which she did with enthusiasm. Once she had completed those two years, contacts within the program attempted to provide an opportunity at the next level within the organization. But that required a college degree, and attempts to obtain a waiver on her behalf proved unsuccessful. They must have needed someone with that elusive competence in medieval history. But, again completely on her own, she decided to stay in San Antonio, a city she had grown to like, found a job, got an apartment and a second job to make ends meet, and continued to live independently in her adopted state. She has since been promoted twice, continuing to make her family proud. Clint had grown increasingly impressed with his sister's accomplishments, envious of her attainment of such a degree of independence living so far from her family.

While Clint often remarked at how much his younger sister had matured in San Antonio, those first two years with City Year were not without some serious adversities, one in particular. Not far from her home, the car she was driving was T-boned by another car traveling at high speed. The car she was driving was obliterated and ended up rolled over in an intersection. The closest car was being driven by a man who was driving his wife to the emergency room. Nonetheless, he stopped and told his wife he must call 911 and approach the vehicle to see if anyone had survived. He later told me on the phone—in halting and broken English—that he did not expect to find anyone alive in Carly's vehicle. And the police later confided that they commonly expect to encounter fatalities from such violent collisions. But miraculously she had survived, hanging from what had become the top of the car in her seatbelt harness. We were stunned by our extraordinary luck. We didn't dare stop to ask why our daughter had survived when others may not have. We simply counted our blessings. But now, as we try to process what happened to our son, Clint, on the night of April 26, 2014, the random, violent, finality of it, we can't help but ask why. The search for "why," the search for explanations of the consequences of violent incidents—these are simply not within the permitted comprehension of mortals.

Carly and Clint's igloo at Rockwood

Clint and Carly at Rockwood

Carly and Clint in the backyard at Rockwood

Carly and Clint at Seabrook

Clint and Carly at Seabrook Island's North Beach with Lucky and Elvis

THIRTEEN

Untouchable Heroes

"'As iron sharpens iron, so one man sharpens another' (Proverbs 27:17). I believe this scripture captures who Clint was."

—NEIL WALKER, Clint's friend,
in his May 12, 2014, eulogy in Pittsburgh

Ihope you recognize by now that this is not intended to be a book exclusively about our son. As you have read these pages, I hope that you have been thinking about your own children or grandchildren. I hope you can insert your anecdotes for mine and for Clint's. I hope we can all learn a lesson or two from a twenty-seven-year life, or reinforce some we already knew.

But my greatest hope is that all of us will renew our commitments to our most precious resources and will express to them our unqualified love. If you already are expressing that love, consider doing it more frequently. If you already are hugging those you love, consider giving them an extra hug. One of the few absolutes I can offer from our endless nightmare is that we find peace in our certainty that Clint knew, appreciated, and proclaimed freely the unqualified love in which he and his parents were—and always will be—reciprocally immersed.

And do not hesitate to regard your children as heroes, just as you would like them to regard you. As they mature, perhaps in an enhanced version of your image and perhaps not, remain open to the possibility of learning from them. In fact, like Clint, we should never lose the child in us.

Clint's favorite preschool friend always marveled at how successful Clint was in the magical game of hide-and-seek (even though Clint always cheated by asking him to yell when he was hidden). The youngster never tired of playing the game with his buddy Clint and now wonders where he must be hiding. They will miss each other.

As I cleaned out Clint's desk, I found a pad on which he had written a number of quotes about life that apparently inspired him (see page 73). Among them is a stunningly prescient quote from one of his favorite books, *Born to Run*, by Christopher McDougall: "The heroes of the past are untouchable, protected forever by the fortress door of time."

Clint, my hero and my son, you are now *Untouchable*, protected forever by the fortress door of time. That door closed way too early, but your extraordinary life, your contagious enthusiasm for each new day, and the galvanizing joy you shared with us are now *Untouchable* and protected, undisturbed forever.

Love,
Dad

*"My dad's the best guy that ever lived. Not because he's my dad, but be-
cause he's the best guy that ever lived."*
                                            —*Clint's iPhone note, February 22, 2013*

LYRICS

We know you had the time of your life

Clint and Oliver (Walker)

In the late 1970s and early 1980s—years before Clint was born—I wrote some songs that I ultimately had recorded by some musician friends and self-published into an album. When Clint was old enough to begin what would become a fervent interest in popular music, I exposed him to my album. I was never sure what he thought of my music (it was certainly "dated" by the time Clint listened to it), but I think he was intrigued that I was able to do it. Eventually, I think it was a motivation for him to learn to play the guitar, which was a work-in-progress during his last years. I know that he occasionally played some of my songs to friends, although I was never certain whether it was to praise me or to

147

ridicule me (he had a talent for accomplishing both in the same sentence).

As I thumbed through the music on his iPhone after his death, I noticed that he had included one of my songs in his library. It was the first song I ever wrote and certainly the simplest. But when I noticed it on his iPhone, I was touched that he would save a song that instantly reconnected us through lyrics that transcended the decades—"I'm Gonna Miss You." My thoughts then moved me to recall another song that I had written during that same period, one of the better ones on the album, which conveyed the passion of a father for a son merely by changing the gender of the lyrics—"[S]he's a Star."

Following are the lyrics of these two songs (and another much more recent one) as a further tribute to Clint and the magical ways in which our lives remain intertwined.

"I'm Gonna Miss You"

Clint with Barney and Elvis at Rockwood

I woke up in the morning light
And you were not out of mind
You were just out of sight
And all I've got to say is . . .
I'm gonna miss you.

And when I woke up I realized
That I never had a chance
Just to look in your eyes
And say I'll miss you so.
I'm gonna miss you.

I'm gonna miss you in the evening
When the spirit is low
And there's no place to go.

149

And tho my tears won't show . . .
I'm gonna miss you.

I know you had to go
But I wanted to say
And I want you to know
I'm gonna miss you so.
Oh, I'm gonna miss you.

From the album *Words and Music,* by Don Seymour, © 1981 Don Seymour, Second Sun Music Co. (BMI)

"He's a Star"

He's a Star
And wherever he is, they'll see what I've seen
And whoever he's with, they'll know what I mean
When I say he's a Star.

He's a Star
And I always believed he'd mean this much
Knew some day he'd be gone but I'd be touched
By the hands of a Star.

[Chorus:]
He's a Star from way back when
I can't see him but he's still my friend

I know it now and I knew it then
He'll be a Star forever more.

He's a Star to everyone he meets
He's a champ who can't be beat
Always ends up landin' on his feet
He'll be a Star forever more.

He's a Star
Ever since I've been touched, never been the same
He's the only one named in my hall of fame
So you know he's a Star . . .

He's a Star
Everyone who knows him will agree
And I'm glad to know how it feels to be
In the arms of a Star.

[repeat chorus]

He's a Star
Even tho you won't see his name in lights
He's had lots of reviews on openin' nights
And they say he's a Star.

I know I'll go far with things that he taught me
Know he hasn't forgot me
He'll still be my Star.

He's a Star
He's in jeans turnin' heads, turnin' smiles from frowns
He's at peace when the others bring in clowns

That's just him, he's a Star.
That's just him, he's a Star [repeat to fade].

Adapted from the song "She's a Star" (lyrics revised to male gender). From the album *Words and Music*, by Don Seymour, © 1981 Don Seymour, Second Sun Music Co. (BMI)

On November 26, 2014 (the day before Thanksgiving), I was awakened suddenly at 6:28 a.m., and a song—complete with title, lyrics, and music—had been written in my mind. I went to my computer and wrote it down so I would not forget it. I recognize that levels and types of "spirituality" vary among all of us who share this planet. But I can tell you that I was not the author of the lyrics or the music. Perhaps its derivation can bring us all strength and inspiration of our own choosing. For me, it will be another cherished reminder of the boundless bond between Clint and me.

"Never Over"

You can brush away the tears when it's over.
You can say it's incomplete, it can't be over.
When the poet writes the last word,
When the chorus sings the last chord,
When the sun goes down, you say that day is over.

But for you and me, we know it's never over.
We will touch no more, but still it won't be over.
We will go our separate ways,
We'll remember all our days
That gave us strength to realize it's never over.

Were we cheated of the time we spent together?
All we know is no one did it any better.
The sun went down much brighter,
And the burdens seemed much lighter.
And that's why we pray for thanks it's never over.

You can brush away the tears when it's over.
You can say it's incomplete, it can't be over.
But we ran until we dropped,
And we went out at the top.
When we won all we could win, can it be over?

© 2014 Don Seymour

EPILOGUE

Eulogies to Clint

C lint was memorialized at a funeral service in Charleston, South Carolina, on May 7, 2014 (two days after his twenty-eighth birthday), and at a Celebration of Life memorial service in Pennsylvania, at Pittsburgh's PNC Park on May 12. The eulogies offered at these services captured his life with dignified elegance. At the Charleston service, overflowing with 225 guests arriving from everywhere, New York to Arizona, Jim Haak spoke, as someone who had met Clint as a coach and said goodbye to him as a friend. Clint's uncle Rich spoke (through his stepdaughter Margaret Vogel) on behalf of Clint's family members with a passion unique to close family.

Clint's life was celebrated at PNC Park in Pittsburgh at a memorial service organized by Niki Walker and attended by more than 325 guests—lifelong friends of Clint's like Steve Basheda and Ryan Eckenrode; lifelong friends of mine like Collier Smyth, from San Francisco, who had never met Clint but who knew him intimately when he departed two days later; an eighty-year-old ticket seller at PNC Park, teary-eyed with pride over treasuring a picture taken with Clint a few months earlier; a kitchen employee from SoHo who had emigrated from South America and spoke only enough English to tell me through a sobbing embrace that

Clint was his "best friend" because he came into the kitchen to say hello to him every day he came to work. I heard so many stories of Clint's remarkable acts of kindness from people I had never met that I left the service prouder of my son than I had ever been. And I realized that my pride in my son would swell with each passing day. It has.

Coaches were everywhere. My high school basketball coach, Dick Black, must have realized that my positive associations with youth baseball and my devotion as a parent were influenced by a coach fifty years earlier. Coach Kosko was there, and other former coaches like Mark Saghy, Patt McCloskey, John Demas, Bob Mollenhauer, Jim Haak, Tom Walker, Jamie Abercrombie, Dan Goff, Ed Contestible, George Elias, Dan Bowman, Phil Kerr, Greg Maxcy, Dale Cable, Scott Isler, and Frank Ferris. Teammates included Aaron Barrows, Drew Isler, Pat Kerr, Dan Goff, Nick Mageris, Dale Mollenhauer, Jeff Myers, Brad Stombaugh, Bill Leckenby, Anthony Rossi, Dan Ayer, Jason Zoeller, Dan Trocchio, and Ryan Rex. The SoHo gang was there and "Reverend Tom" and Sarah.

In Pittsburgh, three eulogies were delivered by young men who never imagined eulogizing their twenty-seven-year-old friend and who captivated the enormous audience. Their words demonstrated their remarkable, positive transformations into maturity that mirrored the essence of Clint's own final six years. That was not accidental. Neil Walker and Tyler Haak were among Clint's closest friends even though they had not been teammates for more than a decade. But the influences that they have had on each other—originally sourced on baseball diamonds—transcended the sport. Clint and our family have been, and remain, blessed to have friends and family members exemplified by Rich Seymour, Jim Haak, Neil Walker, Tyler Haak, and Brian Seymour, whose precious words follow.

Don Seymour, May 7, 2014, in Charleston, South Carolina, and May 12, 2014, in Pittsburgh, Pennsylvania

Clint would have wanted me to say a few words—with the emphasis on the word "few." I will do my best.

During Clint's last evening with friends in Charleston, he was recounting the enthusiasm he had for his new life in Charleston. He had a new job at Merrill Lynch that he was confident would be right in his sweet spot. He had bought his first home, and was taking pride in giving it his personal touches. He loved life in the Low Country. And he was twenty minutes away from his parents, who remained integral to his life . . . and who lived in a community offering all of Clint's major food groups: fishing, golf, tennis, and beach.

And during what turned out to be his last five minutes, he regaled his friends with his favorite stories about his parents—and there were plenty. I was an easy target in particular. He was a talented raconteur, and like most, he never let strict adherence to the facts get in the way of a good story. And of course, those are the types of stories that portray the strength of unqualified love between parent and child. I will treasure the way he was able to spend his last evening.

But more than that, Mary and Carly and I will treasure the years we had with Clint. A special friend of Clint's captured the sentiment when she said on her Facebook page, "In the blink of an eye, everything can change. So forgive often and love with all your heart. You may never know when you may not have that chance again." I can assure you that Mary and I have no regrets and no uncertainty that Clint cherished the love in which he was immersed. His last five minutes reaffirmed that for all.

The quality of his twenty-seven years of life was truly extraordinary. I mean, here's a guy who attended Christie Brodbeck's fifth birthday party as the only male of the dozen invitees. We were put on notice then that our son would not lead an ordinary life. Mary and Carly and I wouldn't trade a moment of that twenty-seven-year adventure with him.

And our family understands that *all* of us grieve. Not only did Mary and I lose a son, but Carly lost a brother, a bunch of fine young men and women lost a cousin, and hundreds lost a true friend.

The crime—some absolutes:

Clint was the designated driver and nursed two light beers over the evening.

Clint did nothing to instigate or provoke any malicious action toward him (street cameras confirm).

Clint was sucker punched—police term—fatally from the back in a brutal attack that he never saw coming.

We are all angry in ways too severe to be able to express. I can't imagine that emotion ever disappearing, but we hope that at some point, that anger will be joined by positive emotions as we reluctantly proceed.

I feel a duty to enable his legacy to continue to shine.

Clint's legacy started with a decision that he had made to be an organ donor. Four lives were saved. His heart never stopped beating and now lives in North Carolina, his liver is in Kentucky, and his two kidneys went to two recipients in South Carolina. If any of you has an adult child or spouse, encourage them to make a decision—whatever it may be— on that subject, so as not to burden the next of kin to make such a decision in an emotionally charged setting. Those four lives might not have been saved had it not been for the fact that Clint was registered as an organ donor, a decision that Mary and I immediately respected.

Clint's legacy will live in the efforts of many (myself included) to live their lives a little more like Clint. While Clint admired certain traits in me, I also admired certain traits in Clint that I have lacked. Clint has been described by friends as being "charismatic" . . . that's quite an adjective to hang on a twenty-seven-year-old. It's certainly never been hung on this sixty-seven-year-old. But as his dear friend Niki Walker said, "He lit up the world." And the condolences that we have received—without exception—repeat how uplifting he was and what a positive spirit resonated from him and how, as Jim Haak put it, "his smile was unique because it told you he had something else to add—if you could just wait a second. His eyes sparkled and had a hint of mischief; you just knew they were looking for the next adventure." If you were having a bad day, Clint would turn it into a good day. Sounds like something worth working on.

He truly had a positive outlook on life that was special. While he didn't know what life's next adventure would be, he never concerned himself with preparing for failure. He didn't fail often, and he had this inner-confidence that if life threw him a curveball, he would take the pitch, unless there were two strikes on him, in which case, he would attack the challenge with vigor. And those who have been with him on the baseball diamond know that the two-strike hit was his signature at bat. He observed—quite accurately—that I always looked at the glass of life as being half-empty, whereas he always looked at it as being at least half-full. Jim Haak: "He was unique and his own man. In a world of people trying to fit and conform, Clint would have none of it. Clint didn't march to the beat of a different drummer—he wouldn't march for anybody. He danced and glided through life. He left stress, structure, and the hamster wheel to us less fortunate and celebrated life on its own terms."

That's another legacy I can work on.

Another more tangible legacy is our creation of the Clint Seymour "Play Ball" Fund. Merrill Lynch will serve as the custodian of the contributed funds, which can be sent to the Merrill Lynch office at 200 Meeting Street, Charleston, South Carolina 29401. It already has received its first contributions. Mary and I intend to match every memorial contribution made this year, no matter how large or small. Its mission will be to enhance the lives of young people through positive youth baseball programs and experiences. We already have some concrete ideas that would please Clint immensely. My goal is simple. I want the world to know that Clint will accomplish more after his death than his killer did in his lifetime.

I know that Clint would want me to share with all of you the deep and enduring impact that his experiences with baseball had upon his life. He was fortunate enough to compete at a very high level of amateur baseball. His team from Pittsburgh won two consecutive amateur baseball national championships. He played Division I baseball on a four-year scholarship at Eastern Kentucky. But baseball influenced his life in many more ways than the box scores would indicate, since he was fortunate enough to be surrounded by the positive influences of quality teammates and coaches who were interested in developing life lessons in addition to baseball skills.

I would like everyone here who had been a teammate of Clint's—baseball, basketball, soccer, or hockey—to accept Clint's thanks for the gift of being a teammate. And I would like all those who have coached Clint in any sport at any level to accept Clint's thanks for the gift of being a coach and interspersing life coaching with athletic coaching.

If I can plagiarize shamelessly once more from my friend and Clint's friend, Jim Haak—he said to Mary and me:

"You were the perfect parents for Clint and no one could have done a better job. You allowed Clint to be himself where others may have forced him into a preconceived model of what he should be. You saw him as the free spirit he was, and allowed him to mature and grow on his time-line, not the measuring stick of others; and you were rewarded for it by the kind, caring young man he became."

Amen, my friend.

To all of you, I say that if losing a child is a parent's worst nightmare, no parent could be supported by a more wonderful and loving group of family and friends than those gathered with us today. Mary and Carly and I ask all of you to hang tough with us. We will need you. May God bless us all as we give our children an extra hug.

JIM HAAK, MAY 7, 2014, CHARLESTON, SOUTH CAROLINA

To Don, Mary, and Carly: We need to thank you both for allowing us to share and participate in some small fashion in Clint's amazing life since we met him as an eight-year-old playing baseball. We all dearly loved him and will miss him.

Clint loved you and was extremely fortunate to be blessed with you, the perfect parents for Clint. No one could have done a better job. You allowed Clint to be himself, where others may have forced him into a preconceived model of what he should be. You saw Clint as the free spirit that he was, and allowed him to mature and grow on his timeline, not the measuring stick of others; and you were rewarded for it by the kind, caring young man he became. You should be extremely proud of the job that you did. Of all the kids I met and worked with, I enjoyed Clint the most because he was the most different and didn't much care what anyone else thought. I loved that about him—Clint was my Dude.

The time we shared with the boys, from twelve to sixteen years old, was the most rewarding and enjoyable period of my life, and Clint was a major reason for that. I think of those times often and never without smiling, nodding, and knowing we did something we could all be proud of. I loved to watch Clint hit, but my favorite memories of Clint were not on the ball field. Clint would never pass up an adventure, and white-water rafting certainly qualified. Showing up with white garden gloves and goggles didn't help much on the river, but definitely added to the legend. The fact that you informed me, as we were loading the van, that Clint wasn't much for swimming, but to do the best you can, further enhanced it. The trip went off like clockwork with Clint and me thrown out on the same rapid. Don, you were always a great evaluator of talent, and you didn't let me down with your evaluation of Clint's swimming prowess. Of the dozens of trips we took and hundreds of games we played, Clint and I spoke about the rafting trip, running on the field at the "Big House," the buffet in South Carolina, and the many other soirees we shared far more than any baseball memory. Thank you for allowing me to share in that.

That Clint and I maintained a relationship past the Steel City Wildcats is a testament to our time together. I looked forward to seeing Clint at SoHo, or out at the house, or out with Ty, and also spent an epic weekend together at Neil's bachelor party that we spoke about often. Due to the marvels of modern technology, rarely would a week pass without him touching base. Of all the phone calls, emails, and texts that you receive in today's world, when I saw Clint Seymour pop up I immediately smiled and chuckled. Before even opening, I knew my day was about to get a little better, as Clint was sure to have a different perspective than the next guy. I traded texts with Clint last week when he invited Ty and me down for his housewarming party, and he promised to serve up Yinzer-Rita's in our honor. When I replied, "Who says I can't make it?" he excitedly replied in true Clint fashion: "That would be epic—hop on Breen's jet and get down here."

When thinking of Clint, I'll always remember just how good-looking he was, and he was strong, fit, and always in great shape. He had a beautiful smile that immediately forced you to smile back, but his smile was also unique because it told you he had something else to add—if you could just wait a second. His eyes sparkled and had a hint of mischief; you just knew they were looking for the next adventure. But if I could take anything away from my time with Clint Seymour and incorporate it into my life, it would be his spirit and love of life. I would hope to one day be described as a character, but feel I am falling short; Clint was nothing if not a character. He was unique and his own man. In a world of people trying to fit in and conform, Clint would have none of it. Clint didn't march to the beat of a different drummer—Clint wouldn't march for anybody. He danced and glided through life. I much admired Clint's approach to life. He left stress, structure, and the hamster wheel to us less fortunate and celebrated life on his terms. He did what he wanted to do when he wanted to do it and with the lucky ones that he chose to do it with; thankfully, I was occasionally invited. He didn't operate under anyone else's rules, wristwatch, calendar, or "to do" list. Over these past few days Clint has allowed me to gain this valuable perspective and left me behind this map—this gift that I hope to share with my family and friends. And I vow to channel my inner "Clint Seymour" moving forward. Clint, we will miss—but not forget—you. "Take a deep breath and put your good swing on one, 24." Love you always, my Dude.

RICHARD A. SEYMOUR (CLINT'S UNCLE), MAY 7, 2014,
CHARLESTON, SOUTH CAROLINA (READ BY RICH'S
STEPDAUGHTER MARGARET VOGEL)

Today Clint will be laid to rest peacefully under a huge mulberry tree, reminiscent of the mulberry tree that flourished outside Nonny and Poppy's bedroom window. He will be surrounded by magnificent live oaks and peaceful tidal marshes teeming with life and representative of the Low Country landscape that Clint had only recently come to love. That mulberry tree will bear the sweetest fruit that will attract birds and deer that will keep Clint company and watch over him. Please take comfort in that knowledge.

Not many people have experienced the pain each of you has felt and are still feeling today over this senseless tragedy. But over time, hopefully the positives that he brought into your lives—the countless times he made you smile or laugh, the pride you felt at his accomplishments—maybe someday these memories will outweigh the grief you are feeling today. Someday maybe the realization of the positive impact that Clint had on his teammates, coaches, friends, and coworkers as evidenced by the genuine outpouring of sentiment you have received—maybe someday this realization will help you forget this tragedy. Someday maybe the thought of the several lives that Clint saved and extended by his generous act of being an organ donor—maybe someday that will provide you solace. And someday in the future, seeing all the young lives enhanced by the good deeds yet to be accomplished by the "Play Ball" Fund—maybe someday the pride you will feel will finally allow you to overcome the enormity of this loss.

Finally, Don, as one brother to another, please don't allow this senseless tragedy to consume you. Continue to make us all laugh with your self-deprecating humor, regale us with your stories, share the beauty you see in nature through your marvelous photographs. Always be the kind, generous, supportive, responsible, and loving husband, father, uncle, and brother to each of us remaining and who Clint came to know so well.

Neil Walker, May 12, 2014, Pittsburgh, Pennsylvania

First and foremost I want to personally thank everyone for making it a priority to be here today. Although a somber occasion, in one way or another Clint had touched our lives, and this is such a great way to celebrate the legacy of a wonderful man.

My name is Neil Walker and I have known Clint almost twenty years as well as Tyler has, and from the first time I saw Clint, which was in a Mt. Lebanon uniform in a summer tournament in Upper St. Clair when we were about nine or ten, I knew there was something special about the spunky, big-eared power hitter from the South Hills. In my profession there is a certain level of player that exudes extreme confidence in everything that he does. Clint Seymour was undoubtedly one of these people. He lived his life without regret and as if he didn't care who was watching. To me that is very admirable. Moving forward and getting to play with Clint on the Steel City Wildcats allowed me to see these characteristics firsthand. Like his life, he played every pitch and inning as though it could be his last, evident by the fact that I believe he led all of AAU baseball in one of the seasons in most helmets broken and batting gloves destroyed. But that was Clint in a nutshell; everything he did he did with conviction, tireless effort, passion, confidence, and with a goal in mind to be the absolute best he could be.

Proverbs 27:17 says "As iron sharpens iron, so one man sharpens another." I believe this scripture captures who Clint was. Fast-forwarding to the man Clint grew into, I got to be involved in so many moments and memories with him that I will carry on with me throughout the rest of my life. Clint made me a better person. On the baseball field, we pushed each other to be the best; off the field, everything he was involved in he wanted to be the best at—running, fishing, golfing, bartending, caddying, being a financial advisor—and that tireless effort flowed into the people that surrounded him to push themselves to be the best that they can be. Clint and I would always badger Ty about the fact that he didn't play golf, and on the golf course was where Clint's character really came out. He just couldn't understand why it was so hard to hit a small white ball straight, but his pursuit to master golf is still ongoing, and I know that right now he is probably playing golf in heaven, without a 5- and 7-iron because they are in the pond on the sixth hole, and he absolutely has a smile on his face the entire time.

Of the more recent memories that I had with Clint, the thing that I know my wife, Niki, and Tyler and I enjoyed the most was our roundtable sessions while having a drink and playing cards. Our conversations would go everywhere, from music, to women, to sports, to work, to cooking. I can still hear Clint's booming, hysterical laugh and his unfiltered, not always politically correct, but almost always true, opinions on our subjects. I have this still-image picture of a pizza cook-off that went down in my kitchen in Florida during spring training that is permanently stuck in my brain: Clint, Tyler, and Niki furiously trying to put together the best pizzas they could for nothing more than bragging rights. The laugh, the love, the joy of that moment and many more moments like that really makes me appreciate the time I got to spend with Clint. Clint's last trip was to

Florida to spring training for several days. He and Don drove down together from Charleston, and Don said to me that that nine-hour drive both ways was something that he will cherish forever. They spoke of his new job, his new home, finances, his mom, Mary, his sister, Carly, and, undoubtedly, how slow Don was driving.

It's evident by this wonderful turnout how much Clint meant to all of us, and what I keep thinking is that God must have really needed him to take him so young. I know he is up there looking over the marsh at a beautiful sunset with a line in the water trying to catch redfish, and that makes me happy. We all have shared such great memories today of a great man, friend, son, brother, cousin, and nephew, but the thing I think we can take away from Clint's legacy is simply this: Live every day to its fullest; love like Clint did, unconditionally and with all of your heart; smile and laugh as much as you can; and appreciate what you have. And Don, Mary, and Carly, Clint loved you guys more than you could know. You raised an amazing man who will be with you and all of us in spirit for the rest of our time, and I hope that brings you some comfort.

Tyler Haak, May 12, 2014, Pittsburgh, Pennsylvania

First and foremost, I should say that we are completely honored to have the opportunity to speak today on behalf of Clint's legacy. Neil and I have gone back and forth on the best way to do this for a week now, and there really are no answers for it, but it's been great to have one another as a support system. As you can tell, one thing we've done for the occasion is grow out our beards as a show of solidarity.

For those of you who don't know me, my name is Ty

Haak. I have known Clint for close to twenty years, which is pretty hard to believe. He and I grew up playing baseball together on the greatest team in AAU baseball history—the Steel City Wildcats. The Cats won a lot of tournaments, and even more baseball games. In 2000, the Cats went 52–12, batted .403 as a team, and finished sixth in the nation—the best team north of the Mason-Dixon Line. In 2001, the Cats won the Beast of the East Tournament (probably Clint's best tournament ever). In 2014, the Cats are the undisputed champion of the receding hairline.

You may have assumed that I was asked to speak today because I am the most articulate and intelligent remaining member of the Steel City Wildcats, and while that would be an extremely fair and reasonable assumption, it's not the case. I asked for this opportunity, as I want nothing more than to celebrate Clint today. We've all been sad for weeks now—sleepless nights, restless days—and there are many more to come. Today, with all of us together in such a large number, we have a chance to marvel over Clint's life, laugh at the character he was, and learn some lessons from the way he lived. In many ways, Clint was my, and Neil's, best friend, and I believe we are best served to preside over this, as we are lucky enough to say that in the days, months, and years leading up to his death, we have never been closer. Over the past several years, I don't think I've gotten more advice from anyone than I have from Clint Seymour; none of it ever worked, but it made my life much more fun, and I always found myself picking up the phone to call him when I needed someone to lend me an ear. I'm sure many of you can relate to this.

I know that not everyone in here knew Clint from baseball, but whether you knew him from college, bartending, EKU, or anything else, there really is no separating baseball from Clint. Evidently, we are currently in the best ballpark in the world, with loads of his former teammates here, where his father and sister just threw out the first pitch on Saturday. He was truly a baseball man, through and through. I believe that you can tell a lot about a man's character by the way he played baseball. Many of my former teammates are here today, and I have seen very little out of these men's adult lives that I wouldn't have expected from what I learned about them while we were playing baseball together growing up. Clint was no different. If there is one thing that stood out about Clint's game to me, aside from the fact that he never showed up on time and had a penchant for throwing major tantrums, it was that he could hit with two strikes (and Don, I had written this independently before you spoke it at the Charleston service). With two strikes, you have to be prepared for anything, and you are one mistake away from sitting down. Clint could foul off a fastball on the corner, spit on a curveball in the dirt, watch a change-up, foul off a curveball, watch a fastball in, and then once he finally got a pitch he liked, drive a triple to right center field. It's almost like he preferred this.

And it translated into his personal, adult life. Some people may assume that what I'm saying is that Clint could perform with his back against the wall. That's not what I'm saying, as there isn't much evidence to support that. He didn't spend much time there. What I'm suggesting is that to hit with two strikes as often and as well as he did, you need to be carefree, and you need to have an amazing sense of self-confidence. You need to suspend all care of consequence, and if there was one thing Clint never really cared for, it was negative consequences. I'd like to give you some examples of how I witnessed that play out in his personal life.

Let's say you had reservations for a dinner party of ten that was meeting at 7:00 pm. I promise, you've never seen anyone dive into an 0–2 hole faster in your entire life than

Clint Seymour in this situation. He'd be dressed at 7:05, and would arrive at 7:30 to a hostile party, likely including friends, pretty girls, and a guy Don brought who was just trying to give him a job. Everyone would always wait for Clint, and I'd never understand why he had to constantly put himself in this situation. But just as sure as you could be of the way this night out would start, you could be equally sure that the entire table would be eating out of his hand, and sitting on the edge of their seats listening to his stories by the time you left.

I'll never forget in 2012 when Clint and I trained for the half marathon in Pittsburgh. For a month or two, I'd drive down to Lebo or he'd drive into the city, and we'd run, put our headphones in, and talk about whatever. About three weeks before the race, Clint told me that he was going to run the full. Some would call this putting yourself into a two-strike count, considering most marathoners restructure their diets, use books to train for six months, and aren't a 180-pound mass of muscle running down the street. Clint ran the full marathon in under three hours and forty minutes. As I lay in bed midday resting off my 2:10 half, he sent me a picture message of a twenty-four pack of Tecate for Cinco de Mayo.

Two-strike counts. While working in Pittsburgh, Clint saw his share of two-strike counts, and I thought several times the ump was about to ring him up. He fouled off some pitches, but he also took a lot of close ones that were probably strikes. Clint and I had a gentlemen's agreement for getting each other out of meetings. He'd call and say, "I'm really hot," or I'd call and say, "I'm looking to grow my business with online advertising solutions." When most people, especially younger people desperate to make a good impression, get an email from their boss that says "Call me ASAP," they tend to call their boss. Not Clint. I know this is true, because I have an email with this subject that he forwarded to me with the message "I'll pass." Maybe Clint knew something that we don't. As many of our peers dive deeper and deeper into careers they don't like, he never wasted too much energy on pitches that weren't in his zone, and I believe he finally found something he could drive at Merrill Lynch. The instructions always went, "Swing hard, in case you hit it," and "put your good swing on one."

When it came to the search for a suitable girl, Clint didn't take as many pitches, but he sure fouled a whole bunch off.

In the past few weeks, one thing I've heard mentioned over and over was his ability in meeting girls, which was mind-boggling. His reputation preceded him. With my front row seat, while I recognize we're in mixed company, I wouldn't be doing my job here if I didn't explain this phenomenon in greater detail. It'd be like eulogizing Clemente without mentioning his throwing arm, Hank Aaron without mentioning his power, Winston Churchill without his oratory skill, or Manut Bol without mentioning the fact that he was 7'6"—it was that noteworthy of an attribute. He was a consummate ladies' man, and just like every worthwhile girl is programmed to be pursued, a true mark of a man that should be celebrated is to be able to identify who you want and to figure out how to get her attention. He had an ability for this that other men could only dream of replicating, and I've never seen it elsewhere. For posterity's sake, I'd like to make a point of clarification that I was not, as many believed, his wingman. Being a wingman would suggest that you fly at the same level and have a similar pursuit high up in the sky, and that's just not what was going on. Instead, I'd like to ask you to envision a deep ocean scene. Two fish swimming together; one being a large, fast predator, and the other being one of those little fish that feeds off the plankton and debris that bounces off the predator fish. I was not his wingman, I was his fin man.

Girls are fun to talk about, but Clint's skills with people exceeded simply meeting girls and extended to his equally incredible knack of making friends. In Charleston, where he'd lived only a few months, we expected a turnout at his service of perhaps fifty people, and were graced with over 225 attendees from New York to Arizona. Could you generate that, just by living your life, in such a short amount of time? In Charleston, I had a conversation with his friend Brad that I can't get out of my head. What Brad told me was how proud he was to have Clint as a friend, and how special he felt introducing him into his friend circle recently. His tone was one of disbelief, like "Can you believe this guy is hanging out with me? With us?" I can totally relate to that. If I had friends visiting town, I would call up Clint Seymour. If I were taking customers to a baseball game, we'd be going to SoHo before the game, and guess where they'd want to go afterwards? If I wanted to take a girl on a double-date, provided she was just slightly less attractive than who Clint was seeing at the time, I'd call Clint Seymour. He was an incredible person to be around for anyone who was lucky enough to get the chance.

I've spent a lot of time recently reading about what people remember of Clint, and since my remaining time speaking here today is limited, there are two things I'd like to address. The first is Clint's smile. Some common adjectives for smiles might be caring, honest, loving, or thoughtful. I'd describe Clint's smile as eager. He wanted to smile, and he wanted you to smile as well. Even when he was angry, he'd be hiding a smile under a look of disbelief or outrage—I think everyone can picture this. People are not only talking about his smile because of its quality, but its quantity. It's been said that the average adult smiles seventeen times a day. That was never Clint. Clint always, always erred on the side of smiling. Neil said that so well—he said, "Smile and laugh as much as you can." That's what we really remember about Clint's smile.

The second thing that truly stands out to me is how many people I've heard vow to live more like Clint. In Machiavelli's *The Prince*, which is a book that Clint had read, there is a really appropriate quote that I'd like to share. It reads: "A wise man ought always to follow the paths beaten by great men, and to imitate those who have been supreme, so that if his ability does not equal theirs, at least it will savor of it."

In times like these, it's always a good idea to listen to your elders. I can speak on behalf of my dearest friends here today and say that we were blessed with no shortage of great men to craft our behavior. These are mentors like my father, Don Seymour, Jamie Abercrombie, Bob Brown, Ted Drobotij, George Elias, Jim Ellis, Jim Gallagher, Sally Gallagher, Dan Goff, Bob Kohl, Bob Mollenhauer, Bill Torre, and Tom Walker. Of those I've spoken with, all of these great people, with all of their achievements, have expressed a commitment to living more like the gallivanting, chronically underemployed joy boy I called my best friend. Why?

In Don's incredibly impressive eulogy last Wednesday, he described Clint as a noted raconteur who never let strict adherence to the facts get in the way of a good story. This is the truth, but Clint loved to listen to a story just as much as he loved to tell one. He may not have listened to Don about directions, or when to wake up, or when to settle down, but I always noticed that when The Great Orator started one of his stories, Clint would listen with the intent of a kindergartener sitting Indian-style in front of his teacher. So, in that vein, I will offer my opinion as to why we all want to live more like Clint, with a story that I myself enjoy. Those of you who know me won't be surprised that my choice of story for this occasion is an abstract story about the Dalai Lama visiting Santa Fe, New Mexico, in the late eighties. As the story goes . . . the meaning of life is to find your pursuit of happiness.

I'm suggesting that if Clint did anything in life, it was that he pursued what made him happy. And external constraints, whether they be other peoples' time, the word *no*, or back-door sliders, never got in the way. I'm not suggesting that you start sending Snapchat selfies where you're singing songs from the eighties and nineties while you drive—except for Don, I'm definitely suggesting that. One hundred percent. But, I'm inviting you all to find *your* Snapchat, fish *your* bass, kiss the girl *you* care about in public, throw *your* 6-iron into the pond, play *your* video games, and analyze *your* baseball. Identify what makes *you* happy, like Clint did. It's there for you; just take it. Identify your happiness, and run down what it takes to get there like it's a fly ball hit to the track, and you're wearing number 24. Thank you, and God bless.

BRIAN SEYMOUR, MAY 12, 2014, PITTSBURGH, PENNSYLVANIA

Two weeks ago, I lost my cousin, who in many ways was much more like a brother. More even than that, I lost my friend. A great friend. When I showed up at Uncle Don and Aunt Mary's house last week, Aunt Mary introduced me to a few people there as "Clint's wingman." I'm sorry, Mary, but you have it backwards. Clint absolutely did not need my help finding a weekend adventure, and I certainly learned a lot more from him about breezing into a crowded scene and subtly charming the pants off of everyone there within minutes than he could ever have learned from me. He was much more my wingman, my support, than I was his. I believe that, even if our fathers weren't brothers, Clint and I would still have found a common outlet for our playful mischievousness.

I've been thinking a lot about what's happened, and since Don asked me to say some words here today, I've been trying to put those thoughts together into some kind of coherent expression that other people would understand. I thought I could stand up here and rattle off some stories of Clint in an effort to remember all the great times and try to reinforce what a remarkable person he was.

I could reminisce about our fishing trips on the Bohicket and Edisto, down near Charleston. Or the time I took him to his first Drag Queen show down there (at least he told me it was his first). I could tell you about all the times he's helped me out of a jam here in Pittsburgh, the tickets to the Red Hot Chili Peppers, or the dozens and dozens of beautiful young women to whom he's introduced me over the years. I could even tell you the story of when he calmly and peacefully fell asleep after a night of quiet reflection following our grandfather, Poppy's, ninetieth birthday.

But I realized I don't need to do that. We all know who Clint was. We all have stories to tell. We all have memories and shared experiences with him. We've all been telling and listening to them for some time now, and will, no doubt, continue to do so for some time to come. If you need evidence of his good character and positive influence, just look around. The funeral home last week wasn't *filled*, it was *overflowing* with friends and family, the vast majority of whom do not live in or even very near to Charleston, and many of whom had only known him a very short while. In fact, I have some friends here today who met Clint only a handful of times, or even less. They feel the significance of his loss as we all do. You didn't need to know Clint for very long to understand that he was someone very special and unique.

So in the end, it seemed the best thing for me to do was to share with you all a few of the thoughts I've been having. We will all deal with this in our own way, but hopefully some of the words and thoughts I have to share will help all of you, as writing them and pondering them has helped me.

Clint has been laid to rest. His body now lies in the cool shade of a mulberry tree next to a tidal marsh in Charleston at one of the most gorgeous cemeteries you'll ever see. Of course, he has his fishing tackle with him.

Even though we *are* here today to *remember* Clint, and celebrate the life he lived and shared with us, our cherished memories of him, I don't think he's through yet. Not by a long shot. For me, this day, and this celebration is not a looking back, but rather a looking to the future, thinking about the memories Clint and I have *yet* to make together, the memories we all have yet to make with Clint and the ways in which he will continue to play a significant role in our lives.

One perfect and very recent example of this happened just two days ago. As many of you know, Clint's father, my uncle Don, threw the first pitch at the Pirates game Saturday alongside his daughter, Carly. It was my niece Hazel and nephew John's first ever trip to a major league ball game. They got to walk on the field. It will be one of John's earliest memories.

First pitch at a Pirates ball game. I can imagine no greater gift a son could give to his father, or a brother to his sister, especially this group of yinzers who share such a strong bond through the sport of baseball. And even though we would all, without question, trade those gifts for just one more day or even one more hour with our cousin, friend, brother, and son, I know Clint was there, to share that moment with us, with his sister, with his mother, and with his father.

While I can't thank the Pirates' organization, Neil and Nikki Walker, or our cousin Jim enough for helping to make that happen, none of it would have been possible without Clint. He is the common thread. So, you see, we will continue to have beautiful moments, and create new memories with Clint, and because of Clint.

We cannot make sense of what happened to Clint.

But that doesn't mean we cannot find value. By "value," of course, I do not mean to say that this was in any way a *good* thing, but rather that there are some relative positives that have and will come to pass, and we should focus on those.

We know the impact he had on the countless lives he touched and can only guess what potentially lay ahead. We are saddened to think that we will never see what he may have had in store. But I rejoice in the knowledge that, freed from his restrictive, material body, he now has the ability to impact the world and those he loved in ways far more powerful, and more meaningful than would have otherwise been possible.

Again, to relate a couple of immediate examples in which we have already begun to see Clint's enduring legacy unfold: His organs, young, healthy, and strong, have already saved multiple lives, and the Clint Seymour "Play Ball" Fund will enhance countless more.

As an archaeologist, I know firsthand of the continuity of life on this planet. I have seen and studied the unique and beautiful environments, plants, and animals that arise where we humans have returned to the earth. And I know that those environments thrive for hundreds, thousands, even tens and hundreds of thousands of years. Uncle Don, Aunt Mary, Carly, I ask that you try to find some comfort with that knowledge, as I have. Both science *and* religion teach us that his soul and his energy will dissipate back into the universe, and transcend the boundaries of space and time. They will warm us and nourish us in the form of sunlight. They will comfort, protect, and inspire us in the form of starlight, and moonlight, and give birth to indescribable wonders as yet unknown.

In the weeks and months to come, we will see him reflected in our tears. In the years and decades ahead, we will hear his echo in our laughter.

I want to make a brief aside to Uncle Don, Aunt Mary, and Carly to echo some of my dad's sentiments from last week. Please do not let your grief consume you. Your family needs you. Your brothers and sisters-in-law, your nieces and nephews, as well as your friends, and Clint's friends need you to guide us through these murky waters and show us that tremendous good will come from this absolute and devastating tragedy. Most importantly, Clint needs you. Of course, we are all here to help when you need it, as well.

We are broken. It will take time, and it will be painful, but We will heal.

We will be reforged.

We will grow.

We will become stronger.

We will find beauty in what we used to see as mundane.

We will gain wisdom and insight.

We will pursue life more passionately, as Clint did.

We will find comfort in the relationships he helped create and maintain.

We will continue to share experiences with him, and create future memories.

Clint helped us all to become better people, and these tragic events will facilitate further growth in that regard. And because of that, not only will he never be forgotten, but he will continue to live as well.

So as we remember him today, let us take steps to ensure

that he will not be forgotten. More importantly, we must understand that the world will *continue* to know Clint, and feel his influence through us. So let us make sure that he lives on not through our pain, anger, sorrow, and fear, but rather our kindness, our joy, our selflessness, and our love.

One story I would like to share harkens back to our not-too-distant childhood, when we would visit Nonny and Poppy's house (they were our grandparents) over in Mt. Lebanon. All the cousins (whoever they happened to be during any given visit) would run around in their yard, and in the woods behind their house, playing tag, or hide-and-seek, or just going on imagined exploratory journeys to far-off lands. Nonny had this beautiful brass dinner bell with a black handle she would ring whenever it was time for dinner, or ice cream, or oatmeal cream pies (Poppy's favorite), to round us all up and let us know to come in and wash up.

I know she's around somewhere, ringing that bell to bring Clint home to her and Poppy. So, Clint, I imagine you've found them already, but in case you haven't, just keep listening for that bell.

"Clint was one of the good ones."
—*sentiment voiced frequently by his female friends*

"In the end, only kindness matters."
—Chelsia Krejocic

Facebook Farewells

Carly Rae (Seymour): There are no words to describe how much I miss you. Love you, big brother.

Ryan Eckenrode: Love you, Clintmo. I will miss you more than words can describe. Rest in peace, and I will see you again someday, brother.

Charlie Yarbrough: Deeply saddened by the loss of a great teammate, a great friend and an all-around great person. At a loss for words right now, so sad. Clint Seymour, you will be missed, buddy. Thoughts and prayers for you and your family.

Lindsey Navickas: My heart is so heavy that we lost such a wonderful guy. You always knew how to put a smile on everyone's face. You will greatly be missed.

Chelsia Krejocic: My heart is absolutely shattered. I have no words to express how deeply sorry I am. He was so wonderful in so many ways. I know words make nothing easier, but just know that I'm here for you and love you with all my heart, my friend. So many prayers your way.

Dan Bowman: Just heard. He was a great kid.

Jan Klett: God's newest angel. Rest in Peace, Clint. Your memory will live in our hearts forever.

Anthony Rossi: No one made me laugh more during a baseball game.

Kirt Kleindienst: You will be missed by all you touched with your infectious personality. Heavy hearts for many around the country today. My thoughts and prayers are with the Seymour family and all the many friends you have made in your far-too-short time on this Earth. Keep watching us all, Clint Seymour. You will be loved forever.

Raelyn Blake: Funny how the good ones go too soon but the good Lord knows the reasons why, I guess. So long my friend, until we meet again . . .

Misty Brewer: I don't want to accept the truth that an amazing person was taken from our lives too soon, so I'll try to stay positive. Clint Seymour, thank you for the wonderful memories full of laughter, adventure, puppies, exquisite dance moves, pens hockey, pictures of Don sleeping, Goodwill tee-shirt shopping, etc. I'm grateful you were in my life. Miss and love you.
P.S.: Take care of Elle for me up there, and you two try to play nice this time.

Nick Garlitz: Every time I was with you man it was great laughs, positive energy, and good, honest fun. You were loved and the people who had the opportunity of knowing you are truly lucky.

David Owens: It's so hard to believe that all of this is true. All of these posts show what an enormous influence Clint had on so many people. I'm glad I was able to be a teammate and friend with such a great person. My thoughts and prayers go out to the Seymour family and everyone else who is feeling this tremendous loss.

Dale Mollenhauer: The last time we were together you took me out in the boat. We saw a bald eagle, dolphins swam next to the boat, and we watched the sun set over the water. We said the next time we went out we would bring a metal detector to find all the Revolutionary War treasure on the islands. We finished it off with dinner with your parents. It was such a great night and it's even more special now. Clint Seymour, you were an amazing person and a great friend. I will always think of you and the entire Seymour family. You changed so many lives for the better, and you will truly be missed.

Mardiluz Toro: Dear Clint, I know that you will never get this message but I am writing this to you because you were someone very special to me. We shared a lot of great times . . . and I will cherish the laughs and good memories we shared together. Words can't describe how I'm feeling right now knowing that you are no longer here. It breaks my heart to know that I will never see you or hear your voice again, but wherever you are right now, know that I will always love you and keep you close to my heart. Goodbye, Clinton Thomas Seymour.

Scott Henderson: To the Seymour family: My name is John Scott Henderson and I am a 1997 graduate of Mt. Lebanon and a former Mt. Lebanon baseball and basketball player. My father, Scott Henderson, ran track with Mr. Seymour in the 60s. My mother, Betsy Henderson, was the activities director at the high school while Clint was a student. My mother told me just today what a great guy Clint was and that people at

LEBO really liked him because he had such an infectious personality. Always outgoing and always positive. I can't possibly imagine how difficult this time may be for you, but I just wanted to reach out to tell you that I am praying for you all and for Clint. I hope you can find some peace knowing that your son left a very positive and lasting effect on those who were fortunate enough to cross his path. God bless.

Brad Devett: Many memories left behind and a great guy's life taken to soon. RIP, Clint Seymour. You were an inspiration to many and have clearly touched so many lives.

Armiro Rodriguez: You are a person I'll never forget. You live in my heart.

Niki Walker: Thanks Carly Rae (Seymour) for letting me share some of Clint's Snapchat videos that we all loved so much. Opening up my Snapchat will never be the same.

Jessica Simon: A very special #tbt for a very special guy who truly embraced living life to the fullest. Here's to that infectious laugh, wonderful mischievous smile, and so many amazing memories!

Emily Scichilone: Clintmo, I love you buddy. I'm going to have Wild Bill's beef jerky today in your honor. Miss you more than I can express.

Alexandra Williott: Always knew from a very young age that you were one of the good guys. Rest easy, Clint. You will truly be missed.

Christie Brodbeck: From my 5th birthday party, I knew you were a ladies man from the beginning. Miss you Clintmo!

Al McCormick: You were special, Clint.

Karen Weil: "Clint." That meant Eastwood when I was a kid. Never thought any different until a smile, as big as they get, walked into my life looking for a job. He had little experience and I was skeptical of his skills, but that smile, that wonderful charm, even an old lady couldn't resist it. That was the day "Clint" took on a new meaning. No matter how bad my day was, when Clint walked in his smile would make it better. That charm I detected made him a favorite with the customers. . . . Everyone who met him fell in love. His presence made everyone age nineteen to fifty-nine feel special, especially the ladies.

Karen Weil: Today we celebrate the birthday of our friend Clint Seymour. Although he is now enjoying cocktails with the angels, we are going to launch a cocktail—The Seymour—tonight in his honor. If you are so inclined, join us tonight at 5 to raise a glass in his honor at SoHo Pittsburgh. Proceeds will benefit Pirates charities. Clint loved life and we loved him—Raise it!

Gabe Cioffi: Happy Birthday buddy . . . I know you're smiling down on us.

Jim Seymour: Clintmo: As we mourn your passing today, we know that your memories will last forever. Here's to turning every bad day into a good one and to attacking two strikes with vigor. We will miss you, buddy, but will never ever forget you.

Shane Zegarac: Many have said Clint Seymour was a charismatic, brilliant, adventurous, happy guy who could light up a room. Clint was all of those and much more. He was truly 1 in 1,000,000! You will be missed buddy.

Kayde Elvie: Mesmerizing to see what an impact this one person can have on so many in such a tragically short amount of time. I promise to return to that mulberry tree—with Clint Seymour.

Lindsay Nagelhout: Carly and her dad about to throw the first pitch at Pirates game, May 10, in memory of and to honor her brother. Rest in love, clintmo24.

Ryan Eckenrode: I hope you are doing well up there and I just want you to know that we all love you and miss you every second of every day.

Raelyn Blake: Thanks for the sunset, buddy.

Emily Baird: A Carolina sunset makes me miss you more than ever.

Megan Herbert: Clint, we think of you every day. I can't begin to count the number of times that Nate or I have wanted to talk to you, or joke with you. I wish I could walk downstairs and see you laying on our couch downloading music or singing. We miss you.

Jordan Tuschak: With "buctober" approaching, I just think of you non-stop. We all miss you so much.

I hope you are doing well up there and I just want you to know that we all love you and miss you every second of every day.

:)

CPSIA information can be obtained at www.ICGtesting.com
Printed in the USA
LVOW08s1114070315

429584LV00002B/3/P